Montessori Comes to America

The Leadership of Maria Montessori and Nancy McCormick Rambusch

Phyllis Povell

UNIVERSITY PRESS OF AMERICA,® INC.
Lanham • Boulder • New York • Toronto • Plymouth, UK

4501 Forbes Boulevard
Suite 200
Lanham, Maryland 20706
UPA Acquisitions Department (301) 459-3366

Estover Road
Plymouth PL6 7PY
United Kingdom

Printed in the United States of America
British Library Cataloging in Publication Information Available

Library of Congress Control Number: 2009935556
ISBN: 978-0-7618-4928-5 (paperback : alk. paper)
eISBN: 978-0-7618-4929-2

∞™ The paper used in this publication meets the minimum
requirements of American National Standard for Information
Sciences—Permanence of Paper for Printed Library Materials,
ANSI Z39.48-1992.

This book is dedicated to the strong women in my life:
To my dear friend Diane for her support and love
To my daughters Barbara and Lynn each who has been
successful in her chosen career
To my granddaughter Rorey: an up-and-coming leader

Contents

Acknowledgments

I am grateful for the many people whose expertise, support, encouragement and kindness in sharing their materials and time helped to bring this book to fruition. Sincere thanks go to: Katherine Vaccaro, Marie Dugan, Maria and Douglas Gravel, Dennis Schapiro, Ursula Springer, Fiorentina Russo-Cipolla, the For Writers Only group in Big Pine Key, Florida, Herstory Writers Workshop, Robert E. Rambusch, the University of Parma, Italy, Gisela Miceli, Louis Pisha, Bette Weneck and David Ment.

Prologue

When my journey with Maria Montessori and Nancy McCormick Rambusch began, I was a twenty eight year old graduate student at New York University looking for a topic for my doctoral dissertation. The women's movement was beginning to take hold in the United States. Although I never went to any formal consciousness raising groups, my readings, classes and contact with other students outside the home began to raise my awareness about the exclusion of women in my history of education books. Where were all the women I asked myself? Didn't they make contributions to the history of education also?

I knew little about Maria Montessori beyond her name when she was suggested to me as a topic for my dissertation, but I was going to find out. I had never been to a conference on my own, but the American Montessori Society was holding its annual conference in Philadelphia, and I was determined to go and find out all I could. There I encountered Nancy McCormick Rambusch for the first time. She was such a dynamic speaker. I heard Mae Gadpaille speak on the geodesic dome and her connections with both Montessori and Buckminster Fuller. I watched Cleo Monson make sure that every detail of the conference was in place. Her organizational skills were evident even to this outsider. The accomplishments of Maria Montessori and her impact on the United States were becoming clearer to me. I still knew little of her worldwide influence.

Just as I was beginning to think women's role in the world had increased, I experienced another setback. Strange as it sounds I had never been to an upscale restaurant on my own. Dinner at the hotel restaurant found me seated all alone next to the pole while couples and single men enjoyed the full benefits of the dining room. I vowed. never again would I allow this to happen. Women were going to take their rightful place in the world.

On completion of my dissertation, my first inspiration was to write a book about women leaders in education. I would give them their rightful place in history. I toyed with this idea for quite awhile. I even helped form the International Society for Educational Biography where I presented the lives of a variety of women who had impacted some facet of education.

One sunny afternoon at the beach in Key West, it dawned on me that my real interest was in the leadership roles that Maria Montessori and Nancy McCormick Rambusch played in bringing Montessori education to the United States. I found there were parts of my life that related to theirs in ways I had never acknowledged before. Thereafter, I immersed myself in their lives.

I wanted my book to be truthful, accurate and thoroughly researched. I wanted to make the language reader-accessible. I wanted the reader to trust me, to know my emotions would not color my objectivity. I wanted to present my findings even if they did not fit with the picture I longed to paint. I wanted the reader to understand that I would never infringe on anyone's privacy nor break a trust with any of my sources. I cannot claim complete objectivity but I think no biographer really can. These women are not a novelist's portrayal. They lived real lives and faced real struggles and dealt with them as real people do. I have tried to depict them as such.

Now that this project is coming to an end, I have mixed emotions. Part of me is relieved that the journey has culminated in a manuscript I can share with readers, knowing I have done my best to authenticate all of my research and make it available to the public. Another part of me knows I will miss the research, analysis and stuffy special collections rooms. I think in my next life I will be an archivist.

I still have questions. For example, what happened between Maria Montessori and Giuseppe Ferruci Montesano that separated them? What happened in Rome to "queer the visit" between Montessori and William Heard Kilpatrick?

I also ask myself what did I learn. I think I proved I have perseverance. I learned how disciplined writers must be. I learned no matter how hard you search for the truth there are a million different truths. I learned primary sources are not always available to the researcher. I learned how much any writer needs the support and nudging of friends and family. For all of this I am grateful.

Chapter One

The Evolution of Women's Leadership

I love fall. I've always loved fall. The autumn foliage: yellows, oranges and reds dramatically draped over the road. As I pass under their arches my heart beats a little faster. I feel alive inside. This is not a new feeling for me. As a child I anticipated fall with its cool autumn breezes, the beginning of a new school year, the expectation of a new world of learning experiences, different teachers, different classmates.

As I aged I began to analyze these feelings. At first I thought can these emotions be analyzed, should they be examined? I came to realize that in addition to the beauty of the moment, the dazzling display of the hues of nature, inside me fall reaffirmed my love of change. This was not change for change sake but an inner desire to make life better for myself and others.

How does one accomplish this? The five-year-old me knew. She proclaimed, "I am going to be a teacher." And I was. And I am. The twenty-five-year old me declared this change to be too slow. She declared, "I am going to teach teachers." And I did. And I do.

Although more than sixty years have passed since I've been in my kindergarten classroom with its child-sized doll house that was big enough for three or four children to enter and role play, I can recall it vividly. I loved being there away from view of all but the other children, being able to freely express my emotions and reenact my childhood fantasies. I thought not being able to be seen was not being able to be heard, but I was wrong. I can still feel the humiliation of being taken out of that doll house and made to stand against the wall for talking too loudly. My thoughts of the injustice of the situation are as strong today, if not stronger, than those I felt so many long years ago. How could a teacher who set up that play situation embarrass a child for playing? I would never do that when I became a teacher, I vowed.

There were times I was made to feel much bigger than who I was, the shortest child in the class. I was the first in class to learn to tie her shoes so I became the one who tied everyone's shoes. I was able to thread the needle so I became the "threader." If I had only known then that Maria Montessori had already introduced lacing and tying frames for children to accomplish just that task on their own almost forty years before!

In first and second grades I was elected President of the class. Class elections had the appearance of being democratic but in essence the President answered to the teacher, not the class. The only assigned responsibility I recall was tattling on the talkers when the teacher was out of the room. In retrospect it is reminiscent of the Nazi period in which I grew up where children in Germany turned in their parents and neighbors for talking out of turn or Fascist Italy, a state from which Montessori needed to flee because of the Mussolini directives requiring children's and teachers' total obedience to the leader. I'm not sure I realized the effects of this negative leadership style until I was confronted by one of my classmates at the end of second grade. He, one of the ones whom I tattled on the most, confronted me and told me he would see to it that I was never President of the class again. I never was. Was this the impetus which led to my current intensive study of leadership styles and the need for change?

By third grade I began ticking off how my teaching would differ from that of my teachers. I promised myself I would never sit anyone on the drawers of my desk because they were not behaving. This was abhorrent behavior for anyone but especially for a teacher. Fourth through sixth grades saw the advent of the spelling bee, another method of embarrassing children who could not spell and singling out children who by chance of birth were born spellers. I was in the latter group but always felt the shame of the others. Could this have been the beginning of the development of my social conscience?

My fifth grade teacher went one better than the ones before her. She sat the students in rows by how well they had performed on the mathematics exam each week, so that anyone coming into the room could easily identify who had done poorly on the test by looking at the child in the last row last seat. Unbeknownst to me, more than thirty years prior to this Montessori had already written in her first publication about the detrimental effects of prizes and punishment on the progress of humankind. The ten-year-old me knew instinctively I had a major task ahead of me. I needed to change teaching. Teaching became a choice for me not a limitation set by the time of my birth when becoming a teacher or a nurse were the proscribed professions for women. Are the choices we make as children reflective of the people we become as adults? Was Maria Montessori's decision not to allow late nineteenth society to dictate her choice of profession what initially attracted me to her?

Did Nancy McCormick Rambusch's insights into the need for educational change in this country resonate with my younger self?

I would like to think that my awareness of the need for educational change and leadership, which expanded over the years and has continued for another six decades, had its roots in my early childhood years when my social conscience was being formed.

I continued questioning the concepts of change and its relationship to leadership. I raised questions: What is change? Is it always beneficial? Can change take place without leadership? I explored the issues of process and product relative to leadership and change. I began examining these same issues from a different perspective. Are there differences in women's concepts of leadership and change as opposed to men's? Do women view the ideas of process and product differently from that of men? I began to delve into biographies of women to see if I could find a link between women's leadership styles and societal change.

The past decade has witnessed a spate of feminist biographies. These biographies have served different purposes. Initially women viewed themselves as a product; one that had to be added to history books, list of artists, musicians and writers so that women's accomplishments (the products) would not go unnoticed. Feminist biography tended to reinforce the same product oriented approach to women's lives. Women were portrayed as models of the best practice; products that other women can imitate. I am not critical of these biographies because I believe they were the first step in the developmental stages necessary to provide an understanding of women's role in the growth of society. Phyllis Rose, noted feminist biographer, tells how as a child she read voraciously the one or two biographies of women that were available in her library searching for women who had accomplished notable deeds so she could identify with women's vital skills and abilities. She wanted to know what the prospect was for a successful life as a woman. She wrote, "I myself was ambitious. I wanted to be a cowgirl. I was seeking something no term then existed for a role model. I sensed it would be hard to find biographies or autobiographies of cowgirls, but the story of almost any woman who had achieved something (besides marriage) would have served . . ."[1]

Many young women growing up in the 1940s and 50s, like Rose and myself, sought out women's biographies and autobiographies for the same reasons as she cited: "I wanted wild women, women who broke loose, women who lived life to the full, whatever that meant. What did it mean to live life to the full? How fully could a woman live?"[2] Even today, many young women do not have role models whom they can emulate and need literature to provide them with these prototypes. These books fill a need but many often neglect to raise higher level questions for the reader and most do not provide insights into the processes that these women used to surmount the inevitable obstacles put in their path by their unique historical contexts and conditions.

To "include women" goes beyond appending women to existent history or adding them as new products to be studied. Margaret Andersen characterizes the inclusion of women as the "complex process of redefining knowledge by making women's experiences a primary subject for knowledge, conceptualizing women as active agents in the creation of knowledge and including women's perspectives on knowledge." Without this multidimensional understanding of the terms, "scholarship on women," "including women," and "learning about women," one cannot fully appreciate the richness of meaning they engender.[3]

Feminist biography can also serve to further the reader's perception of the roots of activism: its passion, vision and personal dedication resulting in active leadership. It can enable the reader to identify with the processes these women utilized to achieve their goals. Understanding these modalities of change and leadership styles employed by women enables the reader to more fully integrate the dynamics and the relationships involved in the change and leadership process.

Women's lives and their expertise in effecting change can be employed as a paradigm to explore the questions of the differences in women's and men's leadership styles and the consequent changes produced by their efforts. In common usage a paradigm is an accepted model that can be replicated. "In science, on the other hand," Kuhn wrote, "a paradigm is rarely an object for replication. It is an object for further articulation and specification under new or more stringent conditions."[4] The study of women's lives and the processes of change utilized by them can be the starting point to explore further interpretation and experimentation in other times and circumstances.

Most people agree that change is not always positive. Negative changes can wreak havoc on people's lives. People who are not prepared for change can and often do experience extreme distress when faced with new life forces. Alvin Toffler described the negative affects of rapid changes in people's lives beginning in his best-seller *Future Shock* and furthered his contentions in subsequent works, thus alarming the public and raising its consciousness to the dangers of precipitous change. Change for many began to have negative connotations.

The tenor of Toffler's first book recounted the multitude of external changes roaring down upon people. His assertion was that these changes were becoming almost out-of control. In reality, however, most people were either out of touch with the momentous changes he was describing or were integrating these changes slowly into their own lives.

Morley and Walsh capture a more accurate portrait of the individual's relationship to change. They explain that temporal change; change over time, produces internal change in people, in their character as well as their behavior. These authors like many other women today are analyzing these inner changes.

In an effort to understand these internal changes, Loughlin conducted a qualitative research study with 24 women who were involved in consciousness-raising groups. These groups of women were aware that they were not in control of outside forces and were examining their lives in relationship to these pressures. In the late 60s and 70s, such groups were a common phenomenon paralleled across the country by women seeking to grasp hold of their own lives. Consciousness raising became the punch line of many a comedian's sharp tongue. Teresa deLauretis, clearly aware of the connotation associated with the term, defended the necessity for consciousness raising. She asserted that although "the expression consciousness raising has become dated and more than slightly unpleasant, as any word will that has been appropriated, diluted, digested and spewed out by the media, [it] does not diminish the social and subjective impact of [the] practice." This process she wrote "is the original critical instrument that women have developed toward such understanding, the analysis of social reality, and its critical revision."[5] Understandably, this process does not produce a singular response by all women. Some of the women engaged in this approach are seeking to re-evaluate and restructure personal relationships. Many are satisfied with their individual transformation while others are moved further to support marginalized women in society. Identification and understanding of the differences in response by these women can provide insight into the change process.

Loughlin explored the process of centered knowing and its effects on emancipatory learning among the women in her study. She concluded that central to the experience is practical application; a way of knowing that includes not only critical reflection but action.[6] Sandler elaborated on this need to delve within oneself in the face of change and feelings of discomfort. She maintained, "Whatever the anxiety is based upon, one of the best ways to minimize the anxiety of change—or any other anxiety—is to actively participate in the process of that change, i.e., to do something." She declared it is necessary to become actively involved in the change rather than passively accepting and accommodating it.[7]

By engaging in feminist consciousness-raising, the women in Loughlin's study were becoming actively involved in the strategy of change and in examining their roles in the process. Loughlin discovered that in the "transformation in knowing from alienation to agency," these women "developed an awareness that change [was] a process of becoming" resulting in their motivation to act for the betterment of society.[8]

McClelland explored the ideas surrounding the activities resulting from this transformation. He addressed the issue of the social implications of power. He developed the idea of a socialized power model rooted in the value of selflessly helping others and explored the ambivalent feelings aroused by the exercise of power over others. The conflicting emotions associated with this leadership style, he wrote, are more likely experienced by women because of their "socialized play experiences of cooperation and sharing."[9]

Almost seventy years ago, Mary Parker Follett defined these same issues of power, change and leadership. Rather than "power over" she termed it 'power to.'[10] Women have not rediscovered the wheel, but have integrated an understanding of power in society. Power evolved to "empowerment" an "expandable resource that is produced and shared through interaction by leaders and followers alike."[11]

Postmodernist thought holds that power can be both oppressive and generative. The skill is in identifying its generative qualities and converting them into "knowledge, action, analysis and energy for change."[12] Many women who came to know themselves and to understand the role of power and leadership recognized the need to develop networks to enact social change. Change achieved a positive connotation for them.

Recollecting their initial efforts, women recalled the establishment of a culture and a climate of change. Meetings and conferences provided forums for women and extended their networks for sharing ideas and materials. Some women began to reason that "consciousness is the way out of the box."[13] Based on historical analysis, some argued for separatism as a strategy. Freedman explained:

"The creation of a separate, public female sphere helped mobilize women and gained political leverage in the larger society," and she added, "Its history suggests that in our own time, as well, women's culture can be integral to feminist politics."[14]

Others appealed strongly for a chance to view leadership and change from a feminist perspective. Rusch and her colleagues contended, "Visions of leadership originate from a dominant white male perspective. Women and people of color have not been knowers in the discourse on leadership. Their voices have been silenced, their presence tolerated but not acknowledged." They advocated the need to view the details of leadership and change through a feminist standpoint theory, replacing "the masculine preoccupation with reductionism and linearity with views emphasizing holism and complex interdependencies." They argued that the masculine viewpoint denied the ability of women to discern their own desires or needs.[15]

Still others sought to work from within the system. They found that systemic changes were necessary and thought these could be made more readily from within. Many believed that basic attitudinal change is often the forerunner to changing entrenched institutions. These women saw themselves as instrumental agents of change rather than passive followers. Leadership often emerged from within by women who had the same needs and who worked together to promote programs to alleviate the issues they saw as problematic. Scholarly research focused on the problems women were beginning to identify. Betty Freidan gave it a name; *The Feminine Mystique.*

Understanding change and the process of change associated with change agents is essential. Knowledge of their strategies will enable successes to be replicated and unsuccessful attempts at social change to be examined more discernibly. Fundamental change requires a novel approach to looking at the situation. Some researchers term this strategy "reframing the question." Schwanke defines reframing as, "the act of taking a situation out of one mental framework and placing it in a different mental framework that fits the situation equally well or even better. Often the actual physical facts of a situation cannot be changed, but by changing the perspective from which we view those facts, we can change the outcome."[16]

This approach of reframing was used by the women's movement in demonstrating the "problems women were having adjusting to their role were not personal, they were political. There was something wrong with society, not with women. And the cure wasn't therapy, it was political action."[17]

It is imperative in approaching change that women set the agenda on their own terms, retaining more control over the outcome. In keeping with feminist standpoint theory the style that most of these women adopted towards social change was cooperative not hierarchical. The process of change was viewed by them "with a democratic lens that allow[ed] multiple perspectives to emerge."[18]

Knowing and doing are two very different concepts. Although many women became activists, not all women who came to know themselves on their own or as a consequence of being a participant in a consciousness raising group went on to make societal changes on a broad scale. Sandler defined societal changes as "changes in the rules, policies, practices, procedures, laws, and programs that determine the course of events." She regarded Eve as the first woman change agent:

> She decided to taste the apple, in contrast with Adam, for Eve is a mover and Adam is not. Eve contemplates her decision; She discusses its theological implications with the serpent. She thus is making a considered decision to taste the apple. Adam does not make a considered decision. Eve merely gives him the apple to eat and he does so, without question . . . Eve is active and independent.

> Adam is acquiescent, passive and unthinking. Eve is truly capable of making change. Adam is merely a follower of others.[19]

Sandler concluded, "If women are to participate fully in the world, they must participate in that world as movers and shakers," *i.e.;* change agents.[20]

In order to attain this goal, education needs to play a major role. The women's studies movement and feminist teachings have begun to address this point. Feminist teachers are providing a more inclusive curriculum connecting the experiences of gender with those of class, race and ethnicity and in so doing have assumed the role of change agents. Their goals, however, have always been greater than the transformation of academic course work. "From its inception, the women's studies movement has proclaimed that changing the curricula means changing the lives of those who study it, men and women, and the society in which they live. The personal, they believe, is the scholarly, and both are political."[21]

Currently many women studies programs are offering specific courses in change and the strategies thereof. They have moved beyond the traditional disciplines, many which presented marginalized views of women, and are exploring questions of women's role in the change process through interdisciplinary course work. Women and change is being examined sociologically, psychologically, biologically and historically. Deconstruction of language is giving women a better understanding of its dynamic function. Traditional courses discuss how women are celebrating eighty-five years of having been "given" the vote. Sandler, on the other hand raises the issue of women being "given" the vote as opposed to looking at the active role women played in obtaining the vote for themselves. [22]

Researchers and scholars in higher education have begun to make evolutionary strides towards change in the academy and in society. These steps have not come easy. Women have been tolerating, mediating, resisting and reframing the daily realities. They have been "professing," gathering data, and publishing their findings and tenets. Their efforts have been heard, read and felt.

Many teachers in the elementary and secondary schools have begun to review and revise their methods and curricula based on this research and scholarship. "These acts of writing are, in themselves, evidence that oppression, discrimination and victimization need not end in depression or despair, but can fuel women's creative and political energies and purposes. This repositions women from victims to change agents."[23]

Traditionally, the term change agent had been defined for and by men. In his book *The Change Agent*, Lee Grossman's first chapter is titled, "MEN, ORGANIZATIONS AND CHANGE." This sets the tone for the entire manuscript. The next chapter entitled, "ANYONE CAN BE A CHANGE

AGENT," describes the historical definitions of change agents. He writes, "Freud visualized". . . the therapist's role with respect to his patient . . . [as] that of change agent." He recounts Lipsett's definition of a change agent as any outside helper who attempts to effect change in an organization.[24] Although Grossman does talk about people from within the organization effecting change, the emphasis throughout, is on a leader/follower model. There is a tenor of confrontation throughout his manuscript rather than an alternative cooperative model.

Unlike Grossman, Judith Meyer did not limit her interpretation of change agents to men; she took an intermediate position on change agentry. Describing the process of social innovation she used the term "control of the diffusion process" to describe the expansion of a particular innovation. She believed "the presence or absence of a reasonable amount of interpersonal communication with an innovation's propagator might increase the explanatory power of a diffusion model."[25]

In contrast, Gergen and Flax urged change agents to "take care to use lenses which prevent the further marginalization of voices." They advocated change agents "identify margins and recognize voices, ensure equal representation without succumbing to the seductive attractiveness of relativism."[26]

The relationship between leadership and change in terms of gender and education is multifaceted. Historically, books on leadership were written by men for men. Although the style of these works was generally prescriptive giving them a cookbook-like feeling where outcomes were pre-specified, the recipes for success were not all Machiavellian. Havelock, for example, in describing the "four primary ways in which a person can act as a change agent," lists in addition to catalyst and solution giver, process helper and resource linker.[27] It can be argued that time has been a factor in the movement from hierarchical leadership to democratic inclusion of constituencies in decision making. One would have to conclude that time alone was not an effective factor, but education and the exposure to women in leadership positions was more likely to have had an impact on the changes.

A perusal of books beginning in the early to mid- 1990's (now available on Amazon from one cent to one dollar) on leadership styles in business, bearing titles such as," *Jesus C.E.O.: Using Ancient Wisdom for Visionary Leadership*;" "*Winnie-the-Pooh on Management*;" and "*Love & Profit*: *The Art of Caring Leadership*," finds the books written by men highlight the need for self-affirmation and tapping into their spiritual selves while the concept of "packaging is everything," is written by a woman. Breaking down the barrier between men's stereotypical "objectivity" and women's "subjectivity, Toffler offers one explanation for these differences in leadership approaches. He wrote, "Today, as more women are drawn into jobs producing for the marketplace, they too are increasingly 'objectivized.' They are encouraged to 'think like a man.' Conversely, as more men stay home, undertaking a greater share of the housework, their need for 'objectivity' is lessened. They are 'subjectivized.'"[28]

Other interpretations of the connection between gender and change and leadership styles take into account the evolution of society as a whole which is moving in the direction of individualization and non-conformity. Toffler believed that as basic living conditions change it becomes impossible for social character to remain static. As we change the design of society, we also modify people's behaviors.

Fundamental transformations in society have occurred as a result of the technological revolution. Both women and men have begun to view the workplace differently. Equal employment opportunity laws have situated them side by side in the workplace. Telecommunications has freed them of the time constraints of being in a certain place at a certain time, and has created less need for face-to-face leadership. This technological revolution has moved them beyond the flex-time developed decades ago to allow women to be at home with their children. It has also permitted men to be at home to rear their own children and to develop different character traits necessary to fulfill this role. Tele-commuting has produced time shifts, with both genders working from home on their own time schedules, thus producing fewer and fewer interactive situations. These influences redefined the role of the change agent in society.

After lamenting some of the negative effects of the new social character such as self-indulgence, escapism, and rebelliousness, Maccoby theorized that education and an inherent sense of human justice encourages critical questioning and not following orders blindly. Therefore, he said, "There is a willingness to give one's best, to be productively involved in organizations run on principles of equity, concern for human dignity, and individual development, based on mutual respect and voluntary cooperation."[29]

The new social character requires a different set of knowledge, skills, and attitudes of the emerging leader or change agent. Youngs asserts that up-and-coming leaders "do not fit neatly into the traditional Western view of leadership." Differences in their styles are the result of "the influx of women, minorities, nontraditional majority males and young adults into the workforce." These new leaders, as she sees it, are being asked to confront compelling issues of a "political, moral, ethical, educational, and societal" nature.[30]

Earlier leaders followed the "recipes" set forth in the leadership manuals while most women who had no role models other than men in leadership positions very often had to employ the male model of leadership. Anticipating this predicament, Betty Friedan cautioned strongly against women accepting men's leadership styles unquestioningly and without exploring the strengths women bring to leadership roles.[31] Heller reinforced this admonition by reminding women what has been previously valued in a leader is changing radically.[32]

In the past three decades women and some men have shaped a body of knowledge which has contributed to the development of new leadership models. These attributes of the new social character include a caring and respectful attitude; flexibility about people and organizational structure; a participative approach to management, and importantly the willingness to share power. There is a greater emphasis on justice and social change.

The positive attributes of women change agents that repeatedly stand out in the literature, include a strong sense of obligation and dedication to women's issues, high activity levels, a desire for challenge and problem solving and a willingness to be risk-takers. "The initiatives in which they [take] leadership roles underscore the reality that things don't 'just happen'; leadership involve[s] vision, energy, support, collaboration and, frequently, crucial triggering events or circumstances."[33]

Although they are willing to put themselves and their beliefs on the line, these women approach their role as leaders with an inner sense of justice and caring. This manifests itself in a respect for the collective and embracing empowerment. They view themselves as enablers and facilitators and have developed sensitivity to timing and the capacity to step back when necessary. These are necessary skills for goal-oriented leadership and suggest the sophisticated and subtle dimensions of exercising guidance.

The leadership research has slowly evolved over the past two decades with current literature highlighting the need for social justice and peace, and combating poverty and marginalization of minorities. These goals require values which have been formerly associated with women: compassion, cooperation and patience.

Some basic leadership qualities are made explicit in the literature while others are implicit, but a distinctive paradigm is not presented as it had been in the past leadership models. Indications are that the role of the leader or change agent has become specialized and requires a contemporary model of leadership. A prototype for ideal leadership should include, but not be limited to, individual character traits. This is essential in order to depart from fixed stereotypes of the past and concentrate on a new vision and possibilities for the future.

Throughout history theories of leadership have responded to the social character of society. When men assumed most of the leadership positions in society, the "great man" or traits theory of leadership prevailed. This theory, true to its name, concerned men and the characteristics believed to distinguish great leaders. Leaders were born into the role. Research placed considerable emphasis on the height, weight, appearance, intelligence, and self-confidence of these men.

More in-depth research seemed to indicate that leadership arose as the result of a given situation rather than as a result of the positive traits of the leader. This led to the study of situational leadership and focused on the primary tasks engaged in by the leaders. One positive factor in this theory is that in ignoring all traits of the leaders, gender was not a consideration, either.

Further research demonstrated that neither one of these theories was sufficient to determine an ideal leadership model. Astin and Leland developed a conceptual framework of leadership grounded in feminist discourse. It views leadership as a process by which members of a group are empowered to work collaboratively toward a common goal or vision that will create change, transform institutions, and improve the quality of life. The concept of interdependence found in feminist dialogue influenced their view of leadership as a team effort rather than an individual endeavor. Women can empower while working with others by delegating responsibilities and enabling others to share in the planning and carry forth the goals of the group.

Maria Montessori demonstrated the power of this model at least seventy five years ago. During an interview in Vienna in 1931 she was asked if she were "fighting single-handed for children's rights." Her response was, "No, that would be impossible. An organization has been formed called the International Montessori School, and I intend to call upon the aid of all grown people who love children and have an interest in their development. I want the assistance of everybody, without reference to political or religious convictions."[34]

Current feminist literature on leadership styles includes numerous references to the prominence accorded interpersonal skills and relationships, shared decision making, and the process of empowerment adopted by many women in leadership positions. Women have always assumed proactive roles in the social, cultural, and historical circumstances in which they found themselves. They established their own leadership styles intuitively and intentionally. These roles were firmly established in the family, the church and other institutions and organizations. Women, most notably African-American women, have found themselves in central positions in their communities and churches. They came to understand and appreciate the need for interdependence in these contexts and adopted "group-centered leadership rather than leadership-centered groups." They relied on teaching self-confidence and self-sufficiency. "The ego needs of leaders [were] placed beneath the developmental needs of the group."[35]

It is clear that social change did not happen by chance nor did the interests of the larger society necessarily play a major role. Efforts at social change originated from women's felt needs not yet understood by the broader society. One of the more challenging hypotheses presented claims that "for many women leadership begins with an intensely experienced wrong. The need to protect their children and families is frequently cited as the initial catalyst for public action . . . by women's sense that they are defending their families and their homes. The personally experienced wrong is eventually broadened to embrace a community and the need for organization emerges."[36] Nancy McCormick Rambusch professed to have come to the Montessori philosophy in an effort to improve education for her own children.

Women organizing for change is deeply rooted in American history. Much of it appears to move far beyond the personal injury motivation. Women have sought to ameliorate social problems by educating themselves and others and campaigning for extensive social change. In the past, they have crusaded for better health programs, prohibition, suffrage, food and drug laws, for playgrounds, childcare centers, kindergartens, and school nursing programs, education for women, child labor laws, anti-lynching and anti-war issues to name a few. Organizations have formed to serve and advocate for women. "Battered women's shelters, women's studies programs, health clinics, law firms, bookstores, theaters, art galleries, publishers and many other feminist organizations have enriched women's lives and furthered the process of social change."[37] They have had a rich history of organizational change models to follow. They have followed in the footsteps of women who took risks in times when their causes were unpopular, who helped bring organization and collectivity to the needs, frustrations, and dreams of unrecognized, devalued portions of society. Maria Montessori and Nancy McCormick Rambusch, each in her own social milieu, were two of these women who took these risks to bring better education to children. Each employed many of these new leadership styles as women ahead of their peers.

Many of the women who helped to launch new organizations for change were graduates of institutions of higher education that had recently begun admitting women or of women's colleges that had formed in response to the demand for equal opportunities for women in higher education. Their exposure to innovative research and influential professors at these colleges resulted in practical applications. Researchers and university professors began to assume the role of visionaries and use their positions to effect social change. Both Maria Montessori and Nancy McCormick Rambusch were influenced by visionary professors during their studies.

Historically, education has been the one institution where women have been able to achieve positions of leadership with greater acceptance than any other. Many women embraced teaching with the hope of making a difference in the lives of their students and ultimately making a difference in society, as well. Provoked by their studies and inspired by their professors, these women graduates were anxious to demonstrate that their educations had not been in vain. Their options were still not much better than their foremothers. They could teach, go into nursing, or marry.

Another avenue was to join a women's club. The club movement, which began in the 1860's, realized national status by the 1890's with the consolidation of a multitude of small clubs around the nation. The National Council of Jewish Women was founded in 1893, followed in 1896 by the National Association of Colored Women and shortly thereafter in 1897 by the National Congress of Mothers, later called the PTA. Robert Wiebe has termed this burgeoning of organizations (men were organizing also), 'the search for order' that characterized American society in the late nineteenth and early twentieth centuries.[38] For women, these clubs were a reaching out beyond the home. Educated women sought the intellectual stimulus they had experienced in college while less educated women looked to the clubs as a source of structured study and culture. With expansion, the club model took on a much broader organizational structure and national outlook.

Institutionalized feminism grew out of organizations such as those founded at the end of the nineteenth century. A comprehensive grasp of feminist organizational structure is necessary to fully appreciate women's leadership because these structures served to restrict or facilitate the process of change. Theories which describe the process of growth and change in women's leadership are useful to provide a conceptual framework of the development in thinking about women in leadership positions and help organize understanding of women's leadership as an ongoing process. It is important to understand there is a difference between management and leadership. "Management is about coping with complexity. . . . Good management brings a degree of order and consistency . . . Leadership, by contrast, is about coping with change . . . setting the direction of that change is fundamental to leadership." Unlike management, which produces plans, leadership involves visions and strategies.[39] The feminist challenge of leadership was to develop organizational forms that empowered women and provided a base for them to carry out their vision.

Without taking into account the historical growth of these organizations, Riger gave a general overview of the stages of growth in feminist organizations. She painted a picture of women's organizations with broad brush strokes, enabling the unversed to see both the harmony and the dissonance emerging in feminist organizations. In the first stage, the Creation stage, there is a lot of excitement and desire for making changes and belief in its possibility. The actual process of development begins before the organization is founded, when the problem is identified and various solutions envisioned.

Contact among the participants is frequent, informal, and requires many hours of working together. In this stage, learning new skills and striving for mutual goals appears to be reward enough for the members. Riger enumerated the many problems faced by start-up social movement organizations. One obstacle is that risk takers usually are idea people and do not like the everyday managerial activities. Others include a usual lack of funding and sometimes absentee managers. Tension may arise because of the financial situation, causing problems between the everyday workers and the idea people. It is necessary to uphold a delicate balance between these opposing forces in order to survive.[40] These dichotomies will become clearer when we view both the beginnings of the Montessori movement at the beginning of the twentieth century and its revival in the late fifties.

The survival rate of feminist organizations is a testimony to women's ability to overcome tensions and obstacles and move into the next stage; the collectivity stage. The demarcation between the first two stages is difficult to pinpoint exactly but is characterized by women's transition from the anxiety of survival to anticipation of results. Job and power sharing among participants is typical in this stage. Some of the tensions from the previous stage may linger, but most manage to maintain momentum and develop friendship networks and shared expertise. Riger posited that different organizational forms can co-exist at this stage depending on the goals of the group. "A feminist group," she wrote, "whose primary aim is to foster growth and development of its members might most effectively remain small and egalitarian, and one that aspires to provide a service for others might function best with some hierarchical features."

Movement into formalization, the third stage, is also gradual and sometimes not readily recognizable by all of the members of the organization as immediately compelling. Increased need for staff is one of the outcomes of expansion of services. This expansion creates the possibilities of newly hired employees not viewing the group's mission in the same manner as the original members or viewing their employment as a job rather than a set of convictions. Once again tension and factions can arise as in the previous stages. This stage is distinguished by formal goal setting, and the adoption of formal policies and procedures but the most significant difference is that the "organization becomes less dependent on the personal qualities or charisma of its leaders."[41] This will become apparent in the depiction of the growth of the Montessori movement in the United States.

Such growth has the benefit of broadening the makeup of the original organization permitting greater diversity of ideas and values. Conflict between the old and new constituencies is implicit in this extension. Kathy Ferguson argued strongly "that an organization that becomes bureaucratic ceases to be truly feminist." She believed this structure "dehumanize[s] and disempower[s] people."[42] Riger, rightfully, retorted that presupposing "bureaucracy is masculine and dominating, while collectivity is feminine and humanizing, stereotypes not only gender but also organizational structures."[43] This process of growth and change is not unique to feminist organizations. It is not necessary to either give up the values associated with humane treatment of others or disengage from the larger organization in order to ensure the initial goals of the organization are achieved. It is necessary to maintain clarity of vision and flexibility in adaptation to the new structure.

The fourth stage in feminist organizational development is elaboration of structure. Typically, in this stage there is expansion and greater delegation of responsibility. There is also a sense of revitalization and regeneration. Usually this stage includes decentralization and the formation of smaller groups that renew the cycle. Riger counseled women to accept inter-generational ideas and added, "Both bureaucratic and collectivist structures are multidimensional, each with advantages and disadvantages. Instead of asking whether certain organizational structures are 'more' or 'less' feminist, the critical question is whether they are useful for reaching particular goals."[44]

Institutionalized feminist organizations, derived from the turn of the century clubs and national women's organizations could be recognized by their hierarchical structures and traditional processes such as elected executives, committee functions, explicit membership criteria and majority rule votes undergirded by Robert's Rules of Order. These experiences proved positive for women because they were "women's organizations" where "women were the leaders, as well as the members, and women made the decisions as well as the coffee."[45]

Traditional organizational structures were criticized by later grass-roots feminists who came to the women's movement with very different backgrounds from their forebears. Many came from other social movements such as the student, native, civil-rights, anti-war, new-left, and counterculture movements of the sixties. Many of these organizations had functioned by the organizational model known as "democratic centralism." The key element of this model was participatory democracy in terms of voting and carrying out responsibilities. In practice, many of these groups, however, were hierarchical and male dominated and women's experience was largely one of being members, not leaders, and of making coffee, not decisions.

Reacting to a feeling of powerlessness, many of the women in grass-roots feminist organizations vehemently rejected traditional organizational models. Three basic premises guided their thinking. They repudiated any form of hierarchy and leadership, highlighted women's personal experiences and insisted on collective process. These new principles necessitated rejection of individual leadership and resulted in rotation of all tasks and organizational functions, making it impossible for any one woman to assume major responsibility for the organization. Although this process eventually empowered some women, others were totally left out of the process and eventually dropped out of the specific organizations and some even left the women's movement in general. These grass-roots institutions, although obviously not all uniform, eventually moved developmentally through the stages discussed earlier by Riger.[46]

Individual leaders have developed styles of leadership that complement the way they view power. Power, to most, is synonymous with empower. Ways to enable others to perform at their most successful levels are jointly and collegially shared by the leader and her co-workers. They believe very strongly in delegation and supporting the efforts of the people involved by giving positive feedback and requesting appropriate criticism. Their emphasis is on process and consensus as opposed to product and hierarchy. They practice the art of listening, but also stress the need for always being prepared and knowledgeable about their subject. "Perhaps one of the most significant skills . . . [is the] ability to integrate their capacities as strategists, facilitators, and communicators." One leader summarized, "And so the craft or the art and the craft of leadership for me is making things clear to other people, not telling them what to do or how to do it or running their lives . . . it's a very special notion of leadership."[47]

Skillful organizational leadership has become not only an art but also a science. Although exact structures and models vary from organization to organization, specific expertise and knowledge is requisite to benefit the community and implement social change. Women have developed strategies that have launched their message and convictions onto the national scene. They have done their homework, their research, their lobbying, and reaching out to their own and larger constituencies to initiate social change for all women and their causes.

Women employed many approaches to introduce their messages. They established their own presses and journals and initiated women's studies programs at universities to bring in the uninitiated. They planned regional and national conferences centered on women's concerns. In addition to providing a forum that pointed to questions that needed to be explored, these seminars "provided women with new opportunities for affiliation, collaboration, and leadership. They offered platforms for leaders to gain visibility and confidence in themselves and their ideas and to test their ingenuity and persistence."[48] This exposure to and from the media required women to exercise and further develop their interpersonal and communication abilities. Maria Montessori knew and utilized many of these techniques at the beginning of the twentieth century. She spoke at many conferences, participated fully in newly formed women's organizations, co-founded others, and published and granted interviews to numerous journals. Many of these strategies were highlighted in what she called her program of propaganda for the dissemination of her method into society. It is interesting to note that although she employed all of these suggested practices, after a lecture which she presented in 1919 she was commended by the moderator on the masculine logic with which she had stated her case. Nancy McCormick Rambusch intuited a great many of these strategies in her effort to reintroduce Montessori education to America and employed them accordingly.

Leland and Astin cite three major factors resulting in leadership achievements: collective action, passionate commitment, and consistent performance.[49] They describe collective action as a process of working with people, networking, and motivating people to work together towards change. Passionate commitment, they say, emerges in people who have been exposed to the values of social justice by their parents and grandparents or have been exposed to prejudices themselves. These people, in turn, dedicate themselves to working towards the betterment of society. Consistent performance has been demonstrated by women employing crucial skills of uniting faculty and students, networking, consensus building and empowering their colleagues. They have devoted themselves to "change, empowerment and collective action."[50] Maria Montessori employed all three of these features in her early efforts to obtain social justice for children and women.

These are the same skills which Ella Jo Baker, the African-American activist, saw as most crucial for social change. She asserted, "I have always thought what is needed is the development of people who are interested not in being leaders as much as in developing leadership among other people."[51] She envisioned leadership as teaching and assisting people to develop their self-sufficiency. She was troubled that as "products of the society we wish to change, we carry within ourselves some of its worst tendencies, including tendencies that will lead to self-aggrandizing and exploitative relationships."[52] For this reason, she encouraged group-centered leadership.

It is clear that women can no longer rely on the male model of leadership without exploring the skills women have demonstrated in effecting social change. Men can no longer rely on the male model of dominance and individuality reflective of the great man theory of leadership as it has been shown deficient in meeting the needs of today's technological society. Betty Friedan, in a somewhat simplistic fashion, writes, "Don't ask what women are going to do. Ask what women and men are going to do. . . . They will redefine leadership. Together, we must transcend the bounds of sexual politics. It demands personal transformation—and involves recognition and integration of the masculine and feminine characteristics in each person. Such individuals make strong and compassionate leader-people."[53]

For an educational historian, it is important to put all of the foregoing leadership material and specifically women's leadership in context. Although this research is not definitive, an overview of leadership styles and processes enabled me to see more clearly the lives of Maria Montessori and Nancy McCormick Rambusch and the roles they played in bringing Montessori education to the United States at two very different times in American history. Throughout my search for what makes an effective leader and her impact on society, however, I always felt there was something missing. Bits and pieces of all the preceding research seemed to relate to Montessori and Rambusch but there was always an uncertain feeling that somewhere there existed a theory that would more adequately advance a style of leadership that I could apply to the Montessori educational revolution, one that encompassed a leader's foresight and her ability to translate this into reality. A couple of years ago I randomly picked up a book which was lying on my daughter's desk; which she had received as a gift and hadn't yet read. It was David Bornstein's, *How to Change the World: Social Entrepreneurs and the Power of New Ideas*. This book spoke powerfully to me of the characteristics of social innovators whom Bornstein terms social entrepreneurs. It once again touted individual leadership. The book's goal is to demonstrate that:

> An important social change frequently begins with a single entrepreneurial author: one obsessive individual who sees a problem and envisions a new solution, who takes the initiative to act on that vision, who gathers resources and builds organizations to protect and market that vision, who provides the energy and sustained focus to overcome the inevitable resistance, and who—decade after decade—keeps improving, strengthening, and broadening that vision until what was once a marginal idea has become a new norm.[54]

Bornstein reiterated what basic logic tells all of us, "Changing a system means changing attitudes, expectations, and behaviors. It means overcoming disbelief, prejudice and fear. Old systems do not readily embrace new ideas or information; defenders of the status quo can be stubbornly impervious to common sense . . ."[55]

Past theories of social change, he lamented, were concerned more with process than with the individuals who were involved in it. They focused "more on how ideas move people than on how people move ideas." He continued, "An idea is like a play. It needs a good producer and a good promoter even if is a masterpiece. Similarly, an idea will not move from the fringes to the mainstream simply because it is good; it must be skillfully marketed before it will actually shift people's perceptions and behavior."[56]

Nancy McCormick Rambusch termed this theory "psychic franchise." I explore this same issue in the chapter on the introduction and reintroduction of the Montessori Method in the United States and term it the leadership in the movement. Grappling with the issue of how to generalize this phenomenon of individual leadership characteristics, which include "the person's vision, passion, determination and ethics," and cognizant of the fact that significant social change requires stamina to remain focused, Bornstein turned to a system developed by Drayton, a management consultant. He divided the concern into four categories, (1) creativity, (2) entrepreneurial quality, (3) social impact of the idea, and (4) ethical fiber, to assess these distinctive abilities.

Drayton elaborated further on these criteria. Creativity has two elements: goal setting creativity and problem solving creativity. The first entails the vision of a new blueprint while the second requires creative solutions to handling the barriers of carrying through with the plan. Both are necessary. This creativity does not appear out of the blue, Drayton contended. He raised the questions, "What's the candidate's life history? Have they come up with new ideas? Have they created other institutions? How have they dealt with problems?"

The next attribute, he says, is the hardest to pinpoint. There are lots of people who demonstrate creativity coupled with altruism and energy. Many of these are good managers and administrators also. The ingredient that differentiates the social innovator from others, he writes, "is that entrepreneurs, for some reason deep in their personality know, from the time they are little, that they are on this world to change it in a fundamental way. . . . [they] have in their heads the vision of how society will be different when their idea is at work, and they can't stop until the idea is not only at work in one place, but is at work across the whole society." One main check of this is to ask the question, "Is this an idea you see growing out of their whole life?"

Unlike the first two criteria, the third focuses on the idea rather than the person. The intrinsic value of the idea and its importance to a great many people is the crux of this element. The last criteria is not always tangible but "requires appeal to the gut." The issue of trust is critical when people are faced with changing their innermost beliefs and behaviors.[57]

Bornstein enumerated six additional qualities of successful social entrepreneurs:(1) willingness to self-correct, (2) willingness to share credit, (3) willingness to break free of established structures, (4) willingness to cross disciplinary boundaries, (5) willingness to work quietly, and (6) strong ethical impetus."[58]

He concluded his chapter on the qualities of successful social innovators with a reminder that although the motivations may differ there is always a pattern. "At some moment in their lives, social entrepreneurs get it into their heads that it is up to them to solve a particular problem. Usually something has been brewing inside for a long time, and at a particular moment in time—often triggered by an event—personal preparedness, social need, and historical opportunity converge and the person takes the decisive action." He added that although it is probably not possible to fully explain why people become social innovators it is likely that we can identify them and encourage them in their efforts.[59]

Utilizing the ideas elaborated by Bornstein and Drayton as a springboard, and incorporating feminist research on leadership and change, I will next explore the biographies of Maria Montessori and Nancy McCormick Rambusch, who were strong leaders and social change agents. I do not plan to analyze each trait individually but to present an overall portrait of these women so that the reader may draw his or her own conclusions as to the validity of the paradigm. Then I will present two chapters on the growth of the American Montessori movement during the first half of the twentieth century and its rebirth in the middle of the century to show the processes each of these women employed in bringing about educational and social change.

NOTES

1. Phyllis Rose, *The Norton Book of Women's Lives*, (New York: W.W. Norton & Company, 1993, 11.
2. Ibid., 12.
3. Margaret L. Andersen, "Changing the Curriculum in Higher Education," *Signs: Journal of Women in Culture and Society*, 12, no. 2, (Winter 1987): 224–225.
4. Thomas S. Kuhn, *The Structure of Scientific Revolutions*, (Chicago: The University of Chicago Press, 1970), 2nd Edition, 23.
5. Teresa de Lauretis, in Carolyn G. Heilbrun, *Writing A Woman's Life*, (New York: Ballantine Books, 1988), 45.
6. Kathleen Loughlin, "Centred Knowing and its Influence in Emancipatory Learning,"(Br.) *International Journal of Lifelong Education*, 13, no.5, (September, October, 1994): 349.
7. Bernice Resnick Sandler, "Educating Women for Change: How to Grow "Movers and Shakers," in *ERIC Document*, ED266694, Eleanor M.Bender, et.al., "All of Us Are Present, The Stephen's College Symposium on Women's Education: The Future," (1984):100..
8. Loughlin, "Centred Knowing," 354.
9. David McClelland, in Frank Braithwaite, "The Challenge for Female Educational Leaders: An Examination of the Problem and Proposed Solutions through Educational and Social Change Strategies," *ERIC Document*, ED280129, (1986), 17.
10. Joyce Antler and Sara Knopp Biklen, eds. *Changing Education: Women as Radicals and Conservators*, (Albany: State University of New York Press, 1990), 279.

11. S.J. Carroll, in Helen S. Astin, and Carole Leland, *Women of Influence, Women of Vision: A Cross Generational Study of Leaders and Change*, (San Francisco: Jossey-Bass Publishers, 1991), 1.

12. Louise Morley and Val Walsh, *Breaking Boundaries: Women in Higher Education*, (London: Francis & Taylor, 1996), 2.

13. Ibid., 3.

14. Estelle Freedman, "Separatism as Strategy: Female Institution Building and American Feminism, 1870–1930," *Feminist Studies*, 5, no.3, (Fall, 1979): 513.

15. Edith A. Rusch, Penny Poplin Gosetti and Marge Mohoric, "The Social Construction of Leadership: Theory to Praxis", Paper presented at 17th Annual Conference on Research on Women and Education, (San Jose, California., November, 1991), ERIC Document, EA024 265: 9.

16. Ann Schwanke in Julia Kagan, "Taking Charge of Change: How the New Role Definitions for Women Are Created by Women," *Working Woman*, 12, (August, 1987): 53.

17. Julia Kagan, Ibid., 53–54.

18. Gergen and Flax in Rusch, "The Social Construction of Leadership," 13.

19. Sandler, "Educating Women for Change," 92.

20. Ibid.

21. Morley and Walsh, *Breaking Boundaries,* xvii.

22. Sandler, "Educating Women for Change," 97.

23· Morley and Walsh, "*Breaking Boundaries*,.3.

24. Lee Grossman, *The Change Agent*, (New York: Amacom, 1974), 11.

25. Judith W. Meyer, "Diffusers and Social Innovations: Increasing the Scope of Diffusion Models," *The Professional Geographer,* 28, (February 1976), 17ff. I made this point in my doctoral dissertation, Phyllis Appelbaum, (nee Povell) "*The Growth of the Montessori Movement, 1909–1970,"* New York University, Unpublished Doctoral Dissertation,1971.

26. Gergen and Flax, "The Social Construction of Leadership,"13.

27. Ronald G. Havelock, *The Change Agent's Guide to Innovation in Education,* (Englewood Cliffs, New Jersey: Educational Technology Publications, 1973), 7.

28. Alvin Toffler, *The Third Wave,* (New York: William Morrow and Co., Inc., 1980), 404.

29. Michael Maccoby, *The Leader*, (New York: Simon and Schuster, 1981), 149.

30. Bettie B. Youngs, "Emerging Leaders: Redefining Leadership for a New Age," *The School Administrator*, (March 1983): 16–17.

31. Betty Friedan, *The Second Stage*, (New York: Summit Books, 1981), 27, 32, 33, 161.

32. Trudy Heller, *Women and Men as Leaders*, (New York: Praeger Publishers, 1982), 149–150.

33. Astin and Leland, *Women of Influence*, 94.

34. Maria Montessori in "Montessori in Vienna Interview," *Living Age*, 340, (July 1931):510.

35. Charles Payne, "Ella Baker and Models of Social Change," *Signs*, 14, no. 4, (Summer, 1989), 892–896.

36. S.J. Freeman, S.C. Bourqueand and C.M. Shelton, *Women on Power: Leadership Redefined*, (Boston: Northeastern University Press, 2001), 5.

37. Stephanie Riger, "Challenges of Success: Stages of Growth in Feminist Organizations," *Feminist Studies*, 20, no.2, (Summer, 1994): 275.

38. Louise A. Tilly, and Patricia Gurin, *Women, Politics, and Change*, (New York: Russell Sage Foundation, 1990), 42.

39. John P. Kotter, "What Leaders Really Do," *Harvard Business Review*, 3, (May/June 1990): 104.

40. Riger, "Challenges of Success," 280.

41. Ibid., 283–284.

42. Kathy Ferguson in Riger, "Challenges of Success," 288.

43. Riger, "Challenges of Success," 288.

44. Ibid., 295.

45. Ibid.

46. Ibid., 232–238.

47. Astin and Leland, *Women of Influence*, 111–113.

48. Ibid., 101.

49. Ibid., 8 and 157.

50. Ibid., 157–158.

51. Ella Jo Baker in Charles Payne, "Ella Baker," 892.

52. Ibid., 896.

53. Betty Friedan in Youngs, "Emerging Leaders,"18.

54. David Bornstein, *How to Change the World: Social Entrepreneurs and the Power of New Ideas*, (New York: Oxford University Press, 2004), 3.

55. Ibid., 46.

56. Ibid., 91.

57. William Drayton in Bornstein, *How to Change the World*, 118.

58. Bornstein, Ibid. 233–241.

59. Ibid., 241.

Chapter Two

The Radical Life of Maria Montessori

In the forty years I've been involved with Maria Montessori and her ideals, I've asked myself many, many times when did I first become conscious of gender discrimination? Why was I so far behind Montessori in my awareness?

During my undergraduate days, I took a course entitled, "Maternal and Child Care." Most education majors took it because not very many electives were offered and you needed a specific amount of education credits to graduate. I remember sitting in a lecture hall with about 300 other women (I don't recall any men but at that time few men studied elementary education). I recollect being amazed that most of the women sat there copiously taking notes. I didn't take any notes because everything the instructor said seemed to me to be common sense. (I guess I should add here many of these note takers got A's while I on the other hand got a C because in addition to the common sense lectures, the instructor wanted to know what the text's author said on the bottom of page 67 or 68, I forget which one). I guess the one statement that Professor White said (yes I still remember her name) is "whatever is good for the mother is good for the child." I remember liking this immediately. It was powerful. Of course, I was going to get married and have children (I never questioned that premise) but whatever was good for me was going to be good for my children, wow.

Eight years later I found myself involved in completing doctoral work in comparative education and needed to live in Italy in order to learn more about Maria Montessori (whom, after completing a bachelor's degree in elementary education, I had never heard of). After completing about half of my master's degree, I had seen her picture on Standing's biography in Indian garb and thought she was Indian. Little did I know then what a major role in my life she would play.

More than seventy years after Maria Montessori graduated from medical school and began to realize the dream of women on their own, I took my children, then five and two years old, left my husband at home, and went to live in the outskirts of Rome. My family thought I was crazy but I remembered what Professor White had said and off I went. Needless to say, I learned about Montessori and I learned a lot about myself as a mother and a woman.

It wasn't until almost fifteen years later, after my children were grown and I had been living my life by this canon that I came across a quote Maria Montessori told to a reporter in 1913, "Anything that tends to broaden the mother tends to broaden the child."[1] This was fifty-five years before I even dreamed of setting out on my own with two little children tagging behind to go to Europe.

A few short years later my awareness about gender was raised again. I was sitting in a classroom watching some three year olds and four year olds playing nurse and doctor. First they shared their experiences with each other. About half expressed the fact they had female pediatricians. When it came time to handle the stethoscope and tongue depressors the teacher had passed around for their use, the boys became the doctors and the girls the nurses. I questioned them in light of the conversation that had transpired previously, but they insisted this was the way things should be. I realized at that point that many mothers and fathers had not been broadened and my educating teachers for change had a long way to go. I wondered if in addition to considering Montessori's life as a leader and change agent could I at the same time look at her life as an example of feminism for women. Was Montessori a feminist? What is feminism?

Are we talking about first wave feminism, second wave feminism or the latest third wave feminism? Or social feminism? Eco-feminism? Radical feminism? Marxist feminism? Post-modernist feminism, practical feminism, militant feminism, or even cyberfeminism? The literature is replete with definitions, nuances, and sophisticated distinctions between and among the terms. Historical and cultural differences notwithstanding, most definitions of feminism contain two central elements: first, to acquire an understanding of the distinctiveness of women's experiences, particularly as they relate to personal, physical and psychological well-being, and especially as they relate to economic and political subordination. Secondly, feminism views designing and implementing collective change as a necessary follow-up to this understanding.

These goals may seem inoffensive, yet women and men alike seem to have difficulty using what Catharine Stimpson, a professor at Rutgers University, refers to as the "F word." Of course, she is alluding to feminism. Regina Barecca writes, "The point of feminism is not to alienate men, but for women to focus on [their] own concerns and needs, to establish [their] own values.

Writing in the *New Yorker*, Jane Kramer described sitting in as a reporter, a non-participant, in a consciousness-raising group in 1970. "I was playing at feminism," she said. She did not associate the word 'feminist,' she admitted, with anyone later than Susan B. Anthony and a couple of "spinster bluestockings" she had come across in the pages of Edith Wharton and Henry James. "To most people," she continued, "feminism belonged to history, along with abolitionism, and prohibitionism, and pacifism and all the other isms of American utopian history. It was something my grandmother had done on the way to suffrage in the nineteen-tens. . . And it was over, accomplished, gone."[2] Montessori, herself, when asked if she were a feminist on her first trip to America in 1912 would not use the "F" word" to interpret her work. We will see how contradictory this was to the life she led.

The writings and life of Montessori, indeed, have had universal appeal to educators. Her private life has remained one of much speculation as the woman who became a much sought-after public figure remained silent about her private persona, reserving her private life for her family and friends. Her public dilemmas, however, she shared as though they were universal truths.

Discussing the division between public and private lives, May Sarton, in her *Journal of Solitude*, offered an explanation which may account for the way Montessori partitioned her life. Sarton wrote, "not everyone can or will . . . Give his specific fears and desires a chance to be of universal significance . . . to do this takes a curious combination of humility, excruciating honesty, and . . . a sense of destiny or identity. One must believe that private dilemmas are, if deeply examined, universal, and so, if expressed have a human value beyond the private . . . [3]

I think for a woman who believed so strongly in the universal improvement of society for women and children and applied her insights in her educational experience, Montessori would have chosen also to impart the lessons she learned in her private life as examples for the benefit of humanity. Unfortunately, she did not. She led many lives. Most of them were radical lives.

Maria's early childhood years at home and in school have become tales that are passed on from author to author. Although most are very entertaining and are featured heavily in children's biographies of Montessori, their authenticity can only be judged by the sources from which they come. There are two major extant biographies of Maria Montessori. One is hagiographic while the other is hypercritical. There is a third biography by Anna Maria Maccheroni, reverent in nature, entitled; *A True Romance: Dr. Maria Montessori as I Knew Her*.

Much of Maria's background is taken from her principal biographers in both English and Italian. Her father, Alessandro Montessori was born in Ferrara, Italy on August 2, 1835.[4] In his younger years he served in the military fighting for the liberation of Italy from Austrian rule. After his military service, he worked for the Papal state in its finance department. He left that position after five years and began to work in the salt and tobacco business continuing to rise within the state-run industry. By 1865, he was involved in its financial management and was transferred to Chiaravalle, a tobacco growing town, where he met Renilde Stoppani and married her in the spring of 1866.

Renilde Stoppani was an educated woman when she met her husband. She loved to read. She was dedicated to autonomy and a unified Italy. Alessandro was a man who could identify with her beliefs. His work required frequent relocation. In 1867 he was reassigned to Venice where they lived until 1869 when they returned to Chiaravalle.

Maria Montessori was born on the 31st of August in 1870 there. It was and still is a very small town in the province of Ancona on the Adriatic Sea. I visited there in 1970 for the centenary of her birth and found a street named after her, a small plaque on the wall of the house in which she was born and a small Montessori school. The house has since been turned into a modest museum housing some of her books and documents.

In Chiaravalle, I observed the actual birth record for Maria Montessori. It was in a large bound book containing the names of many children born in 1870 in Chiaravalle. The details of her birth and names of her parents can be found on the bottom of one page and the top of the next.

Could Maria's parents have foreshadowed the life of the baby whom they had just brought into the world? Or did the educated, forwarded thinking Renilde Stoppani Montessori name her daughter filled with hope that one day she like her namesakes would challenge the status-quo and leave her own mark on the world? Maria's full name is Maria Tecla Artemisia Montessori.

Many myths and legends have grown around the life of Maria Montessori. Similarly, there are many tales surrounding her given middle names. Tecla (sometimes spelled Thecla) is described as a "young noble virgin" who listened to the sermons of the apostle Paul on the virtues of virginity. Threatened by her rapt attention to these teachings, her mother and her fiancée, Thamyris, incited a mob to drag Paul to the governor and have him imprisoned.

Tecla, then, persuaded a guard to let her into Paul's cell where she sat at his feet all night. When she was found, her mother had her brought before the governor again. Paul was expelled and Tecla was ordered to be burned at the stake as a lesson to all other women who might listen to Paul's teachings. She was tied to a stake and set on fire but was saved by a storm "which God sent to put out the flames."

Paul and Tecla were reunited and fled to Pisidian Antioch where a nobleman named Alexander upon seeing her desired her. Paul alleged that he did not know her so Alexander attempted to rape her. While fighting him off,

Alexander was hurt so he brought her before the governor for assaulting a nobleman. She was sentenced to be eaten by wild beasts and was tied to a lioness.

The women of the city protested the injustice of her sentence. The tale continues as Tecla is saved from death first by the lioness who fought off the other beasts and then by a series of miracles where she escaped unharmed and returned to Paul, her mentor.

The authors admit that the narrative is probably unhistorical and definitely overstated and surely sexually explicit but maintain the praise of virginity and the experience of persecution was a running theme in early Christianity. Some modern scholars view this account as a "proto-feminist text." They suggest that Tecla, who is abused by men and their world, still refuses to "conform to its expectations, marriage patterns, and dress code. She boldly asserts her independence, receiving support from many women."[5]

Coincidence? Self-fulfilling prophesy? More likely, historical circumstance can account for the less than equal treatment Maria received in a male-dominated society, but how do we explain the non-conformity, refusal to marry, independence and support of her women followers?

As you will see, Maria, too, was influenced by the teachings of male mentors whose lectures would inspire her for the benefit of women, children, and the under-served populations. You will also read about lions with whom she came in contact and would disregard while holding onto her principles. The lions certainly had to be coincidence.

Her mother, Renilde, would have been familiar with the arts and Greek mythology. Maria Montessori s name Artemisia may have been taken from Artemis, the Greek Goddess of the forests and of childbirth, but it seems even more probable that she was named after Artemisia Gentileschi, one of the most important women artists of the Baroque period.

If her middle name were taken from the artist, it too is linked with sexual exploitation. Although, Artemisia displayed a very early talent for painting, she was denied entrance to the all-male academies of art. Her father, a well known painter, hired the painter Tassi to tutor her privately. While under his apprenticeship, Artemisia accused him of rape and a seven month trial followed. During this period, she was "given a gynecological examination and was tortured using a device made of thongs wrapped around the fingers and tightened by degrees." This torture was administered in the belief that if a person told the same story under these circumstances then the story must be true. Tassi was later sentenced to one year imprisonment.

In order to restore his daughter's honor, her father arranged for her to marry an artist from Florence. They moved there shortly afterwards, and Artemisia was accepted into the Accademia del Disegno (Academy of Drawing). She was the first woman ever to attend. Today she is considered the "the most important woman artist of the pre-modern era, and a major artist of the Italian Baroque."[6] Her interpretation of rape and vengeance from a woman's perspective was a major achievement in art history.

Did these names presage the life Maria Tecla Artemisia Montessori was to live, or did she choose to live up to her names by leaving her own mark on education and social change?

Early in her life, Montessori challenged the social conventions of her day by deciding to channel her interest in mathematics to study engineering. Later in life, Montessori would credit her mother with having influenced her professional choices. Renilde Stoppani had a strong personality, was well-read, held many liberal ideas and exhibited original ways of thinking. One of Montessori's schoolmates described the presence of Maria's mother in her life. "We sat," her classmate said, "next to each other . . . The door of the studio where we were always had to stay open because in the next room, the dining room, a huge matron, her mother, would read, smoke and admire her."[7]

In 1863, The Casati legislation made it possible for young women to enter Liceo (high school) and technical institutes. In October of that same year Educational Minister Baccelli endorsed the idea of accepting young women who wanted more than four years of education into these schools. Maria Montessori was one of these young women. Secondary education was not free at that time in Italy so perhaps because of interest in the subject matter or maybe because of economics, Maria made the decision at age thirteen to attend a technical school, Michelangelo Buonarotti. This early choice would have later ramifications.

Handed down tales depict her in school among all young men except for one other young woman. To shield them from the torments of the young men, the two young women were put into a special room during recess. This experience, if factual, does not appear to have discouraged Montessori but appears to have given her greater inner strength. Her next step was to register in the Liceo Scientifico (the scientific or technical high school). She was unable to attend Liceo Classico (the classical high school), because she had not enrolled previously in classical courses. She was graduated from the Leonardo da Vinci Technical Institute in 1890.

There are varied accounts of the trials and tribulations of her next life choice, admission into medical school. Legend tells of interviews with Guido Baccelli, Professor of Clinical Medicine who turned down her application for entrance. Her retort upon leaving him was, "I know I will become a doctor." Other stories include the intervention of the Pope on her behalf for entrance into medical school.

Still another version is from a magazine article in *L'illustazione Italiana,* published in March 1899 which allegedly was based on an interview. This article talked of the intercession of a not well defined religious figure who made it possible for her to study Latin and Greek as long as she stayed hidden behind a wooden bookcase so as not to disturb the seminarians. This solution did not work because of the sudden death of this religious figure.[8] We can hypothesize here if indeed this story is accurate, the religious figure may very well have been her uncle, Antonio Stoppani, her mother's brother. As a scholar-priest at the University of Milan he had taken many liberal positions on church and state and on positivist science, a field his niece would endorse years later. He died in 1891, shortly after Maria's graduation from the Liceo Scientifico.

Simply put, however, she did not have the prerequisites for entrance to the University of Rome Medical School. Her main deficiency was her lack of knowledge of classical languages because of her prior attendance at technical schools. She did enter the University as a part time student to make up the deficit. It took her two years to complete the course of study and in 1892 she passed and received a diploma in natural sciences.

1892 appears to be an important year in the life of the twenty-two year old Maria Montessori. In May of that year the second flower festival organized by the women of the Roman aristocracy and university students was held in the Villa Borghese. Montessori was chosen to offer the flag to Queen Margherita. Newspapers reported on her grace and the natural way in which she was able to convince the Queen to accept the flag while indicating to her that she was a medical student and a student of the natural sciences. Babini noted that this is the beginning of her appearances with public figures and when aristocracy began to be part of her life.[9] Many of these people would later play a major role in the professional and political life of Dr. Montessori.

1892 is also the year in which, after great perseverance, she entered the University of Rome Medical School. Legend surfaces once again. Almost all biographies, histories and tales of Maria Montessori portray her as the first woman to graduate from medical school in Italy, or some as the first woman to graduate from the University of Rome Medical School. In an article written in 1915 in the *San Francisco Call and Post*, purportedly written by Maria Montessori, she is quoted as saying, "I was the first woman physician graduated from the famous University of Rome."[10]

Other sources differ. In 1877 Ernestine Paper of Florence was the first woman to become a physician after the unification of Italy, followed by Velleda Maria Farni from the University of Turin in 1878.[11] In 1882, Osmilda Ferraresi earned the degree in Medicine and Surgery at the University of Modena,[12] Succeeding them were Giuseppina Cattani in 1884 at the University of Bologna and then Avalle Paola in Cristoforis from Cagliari University a year later.[13] Two women graduated earlier from the University of Rome Medical School, Edvige Benigni in 1890 and four years later Marcellina Corio Viola, in 1894. One year before Montessori received her medical degree yet another woman, Deco Afra, earned her degree at the University of Parma.[14] Two more women graduated as doctors the same year as Montessori, Emilia Concornotti from Pavia and Adelina Rossi from Turin.[15] In a speech in 1896 Montessori, herself, refers to other women physicians besides herself.[16]

These facts are not to take from the remarkable talent or perseverance of Maria Montessori. Although records indicate that many women practiced medicine in Italy before its unification,[17] modern Italy appears to have reverted to excluding women from medical schools. In a book written by Victor Rava in 1902 he demonstrated just how difficult the feat of women graduating from medical school was at the end of the nineteenth century. In the twenty years following the first female medical graduate until the beginning of the twentieth century only twenty-four women achieved this degree. And, only eleven of them, including Montessori who graduated in 1896 in Medicine and Surgery, had enrolled in a course of studies in physics and mathematics. The years 1880–1900 witnessed a great expansion in University enrollment in general and the Faculty of Medicine in particular. The number of courses at the University of Rome had virtually tripled in the fifteen-year period prior to Montessori's entrance into the school.[18]

Many of the legends, myths and tales of the young medical student deal with her working under great adversity, unable to view a naked body in the presence of men, compelled to perform autopsies alone at night without the benefit of direct instruction from her professors, enduring taunting from her fellow students and receiving little encouragement from her family, especially her father, who reportedly would have preferred for her to become a teacher.

Legend? Fact? No one can be really sure, although in 1893 there is a mention in the Italian press of her being the only woman present at the cremation and wake of one of her professors, Professor Molischott. Babini noted this was indicative of a young woman who wanted to demonstrate publicly taking on a role previously reserved for men not only culturally but psychologically.[19] I am sure these hardships made a remarkable impression on Montessori as a person and a woman.

The greatest impact came from her professors in the faculty of medicine. Many of them were left wing and were interested in the new sciences, particularly the pathology of "degenerate" children. As a young student Montessori found herself in these surroundings just as she began to form her professional ideas. Babini described the 1870's as the "years that medicine begins to claim for itself the ability and the competence to enlarge its own field of intervention to the point that it would actually promote a kind of physical, moral and social regeneration of the young Italian state."[20]

Professor Molischott was one of the faculty who impacted her studies. She received the highest grade in all of her studies in his class in experimental physiology. His lectures always moved beyond the discipline of medicine into themes of philosophy and methodology but more importantly he initiated the new discipline of social physiology or social medicine, specifically with relation to the conditions of life in the lower classes. This same interest was expressed by Professor Celli in experimental hygiene, who elaborated on the idea that such diseases as tuberculosis and malaria could be eliminated from the lower classes if the economic institutions actually wanted them to be. These two men also took a very active role in their commitment to schools, children and the equality of women. Their passion and sense of responsibility to these constituencies came at a moment when the young Montessori was predisposed to these liberal ideas. These same beliefs were supported by the Roman women of the aristocracy.

Montessori's interest led her to serve as an intern at a psychiatric clinic. There she would come in contact with Professor Bonfigli, who also took an interest in social medicine and lectured on the need to care for poor and ill children. He extended his lectures to include the social aspects of madness and the development of children's moral sense and character, all ideas which would resonate with Maria Montessori. Her four years of medical school were filled with motivating, appealing, innovative, and sometimes radical instruction. She sometimes experienced great differences between theory and practice.

In March of 1896, an investigative report was published by the magazine *Illustrazione Popolare,* as to whether women could actually become doctors. The results demonstrated great public opposition to this notion.[21] Regardless, Montessori continued working in the pediatric ambulatory clinic and other hospitals, sustaining her relationship with the women of the Roman aristocracy who supported these efforts. She also began her work with children there.

At the same time she was working in these hospitals, both as a professional and as a member of the women's association which had been founded a little earlier, Montessori also worked at the university's psychiatric clinic, gathering materials for her dissertation on antagonistic hallucinations. Her decision to work in the field of psychiatry rather than pediatrics or gynecology, which might have more readily welcomed a woman, and to work at these hospitals, which were usually housed with mental asylums, was not only highly unusual but also dangerous. This choice appears to be based on her passion for scientific research and empirical psychology evoked by professors such as Bonfigli, Molischott, and Labriola and others, who continued to lecture on the social implications of psychological research. Babini speculated that another reason Montessori may have chosen this highly uncommon field of study was because another volunteer at the clinic was Giuseppe Ferrucio Montesano. The combination of these passions may indeed have led her into this new field of study.

Montessori and Montesano probably met in 1895 while she was interning and completing research for her doctoral thesis at the psychiatric clinic Montesano directed. Babini remarked that some relatives indicated it might have been even earlier than that. According to Babini it is apparent by the end of the century that Maria Montessori and Giuseppe Montesano were a couple who were productive in the scientific and social fields. They published together under the auspices of the psychiatric institute and the University of Rome. Both authors were given equal acknowledgment for their research. This was highly unusual at that time since one of the researchers was a woman. Babini concluded that this was indicative of the natural parity that had been established between Montessori and Montesano. Together, in 1898, they had founded a society in Rome called *Per la Donna*, (For the Woman). Its goals were to have men and women collaborate in scientific and social fields, publish together, and speak together and carry on other related activities. The couple's relationship reflected the Society's goals. It proceeded on the basis of common ideals, social efforts and scientific research in a very non-traditional fashion.

From this intellectual, social, political and intimate relationship a son was born on March 31, 1898. The birth registry lists his name as Mario Pipilli. The actual registration of his birth was performed by Mancia Carlotta on April 2, 1898 and indicates that he was born of "unknown parents." At that time Carlotta declared in front of two witnesses that she would nurse and take care of this child. There is no indication of where the last name Pipilli originated. Carlotta took him to the Roman countryside in the small town of Vicovaro, where he would continue to live for many years in anonymity.[22]

Kramer and many other sources before and after her claim that both Maria's mother and Montesano's mother encouraged her to keep Mario's birth a secret. Many claim that Montesano's mother would not allow them to marry since Maria was not the type of woman she wanted for her son. It is hard to imagine this kind of arrangement today but at the turn of the century in Italy it was probably very common. The couple promised each other never to marry anyone else, a promise Montesano would break in 1901.

Kramer claimed that Mario told her his father's mother opposed the marriage. She seemingly doubted this explanation and commented, "Montessori herself, strong-willed and used to overcoming obstacles and forging ahead to achieve her own goals, already accomplished at persuading others to her purposes, must have had her own reasons for not marrying the father of her child."[23]

Montessori's private life has remained one of much speculation. The contrast by Montessori's two biographers in dealing with her private life is astounding. Rita Kramer, who had access to Montessori's private papers apparently wrote of every detail she had uncovered and theorized freely on Montessori's private life and affairs, both literally and figuratively, while, in E.M. Standing's biography, one gets the impression that Mario sprung from the head of Zeus, almost literally.

Mario was not legally recognized by his father, Giuseppe Montesano, until September 28, 1901, eight days before Montesano's marriage to Maria Aprile, on October 6, 1901.[24] No reason is given for this legalization of a son born three and a half years before. Was it closure of his relationship with Maria before his upcoming marriage? Was it the conscience of a man whose prior behaviors reveal a man who supported feminist causes, who treated women as equals, who was one of the only men in the organization *Per la Donna* before the turn of the century? We can only conjecture.

It is interesting to note that although Mario is always referred to in the literature as Mario Montessori it was not until March 25, 1950 by the decree of the President of the Italian republic that he was at long last authorized to add to his surname Montesano the family name Montessori and thus make legal use of the Montessori name.

Although Mario came to live with Montessori at the end of 1912, shortly after her mother's death, he continued to be referred to as Maria's nephew or her adopted son until her death in 1952. In her will she referred to him as "mio figlio," my son.

As to why Maria never married Dr. Montesano there is still a great deal of supposition. Perhaps she did not want to disappoint her mother who had always encouraged her to strive for more in life, who desired that her daughter not follow in her footsteps and become an educated homemaker. It seems significant that Maria reclaimed her son soon after her mother's death.

Or perhaps it was her strong ideals? Paola Boni Fellini remembered that era. She wrote, "This is a period of incredible buzzing energies. There was a strong fixation with detachments from the past, a fixation with renewal, it is a period of free unions between lovers."[25]

Montessori, who had traveled widely and was very well read, seems to have been influenced by these views. In prior speeches, she had expounded on unions of love, of collaboration, of free and conscientious maternities of science as an instrument of power. For reasons known only to her, but most likely coinciding with some of these beliefs, she chose not to marry the father of her child and resolved to take her future into her own hands. She believed social progress depended on women's emancipation. This conviction was bolstered by her own educational struggles and successes. This decision was the watershed of her life. Her private life remained concealed. In public, however, Montessori lived a radical life. The decisions she made that enabled her to overcome the vast restrictions put on a woman born in Italy in 1870 excite the imagination to the unlimited possibilities available to women who choose to write their own scripts.

After the completion of her dissertation which she defended on July 10, 1896, and in spite of all the public obstacles and mixed feelings about women doctors or perhaps because of them, Maria Montessori went on to graduate from medical school. To better understand the meaning of her successful completion of medical school we must not forget that in that academic year of a total of 21,813 people enrolled in Italian universities only 132 were women, a little more than half a percent.

Even before graduation Montessori's energies were beginning to focus in other directions. In March 1896, a women's association, *Associazione Femminile di Roma* was founded in Rome. One of its main promoters was Rosa-Mary Amadori who was the chief editor of the magazine *Vita Femminile* (Woman's Life.) Maria Montessori was its vice secretary and Virginia Nathan, the wife of the future mayor of Rome, its treasurer. The stated aims of this organization were to instill in women a spirit of solidarity and femininity and at the same time encourage them to tend to their own interests. Montessori was beginning to be recognized as a champion for women's rights.

Concurrently, the newly united country of Italy was engaged in a war in Africa to colonize Ethiopia, a war in which they were eventually soundly defeated. Women's associations in Milan and Turin and other cities had already begun to voice opposition to this war in Africa. On the day of its inauguration the Roman Association read a proclamation of the newly constituted International Union of Women for Peace. They proposed working together with women to support peace and to plan conferences and lectures for union workers on hygiene and peace. Their intent was that journals and newspapers should be put at the disposal of women workers with women as the main subject. As a woman of science Montessori made great contributions to the activities of this association.

Numerous women's organizations were also founded in Germany. Several, in order to differentiate between them and the older organizations called themselves "radicals," although they appealed to moderate and conservative feminists by pressing for economic, social and political equality for women. In 1896 one of the major groups, the Association for Women's Weal, capitalized on the opening of the Berlin Exposition to hold an International Women's Congress there entitled, "Women's Achievements and Women's Endeavors."[26] Montessori was an invited representative.

The newly formed women's association of which Montessori was secretary decided to send her to represent Italian women at the Women's International Congress in Berlin and began fund raising to pay for her trip and expenses. There was an immediate donation of 50 lire from the bourgeois women of Chiaravalle, her birthplace. But, Babini wrote, "pledges came from all over Italy and they all seemed to legitimize a candidacy that was not only national but broke every class barrier."[27] Women from all over were responding to the newspaper and journal articles reporting Montessori would be speaking on equal salaries for women. The efforts of the Roman Women's Association and Montessori's hard work were beginning to pay off.

Montessori waxed proud at the overwhelmingly positive response of the Roman Women's Association to sending a Delegate to the Berlin conference. She credited the women of Rome as the "first in Italy who considered the sending of a delegate." At which time, she said, [they] "turned to all women in the country in order to secure their approval and support." She recounted how numerous and eager support was received from all parts of Italy, mainly from women's groups. In one area there was even a men's group which enthusiastically backed sending a woman to the convention. Funding came from aristocratic women, ambitious housewives and some Catholic women, "who although not actively involved in this matter, anticipated in their hearts and eagerly awaited the success.[28]

Describing the beginnings of the Women's Association in Rome in one of her addresses to the Berlin conference, Montessori said, "The women's movement has only just begun to make itself noticed in this city! In Italy, this movement is only slowly making its way over the mountains into the country's interior. As soon as the women's question had found a crack between the ruins of Roman monuments and the heaps of Catholic prejudgments, it pushed itself through in the form of a friendly, modern beam of light and led to [its] foundation."[29]

All did not run smoothly at the conference. There was a protest march by 3000 socialist women calling for the abolition of the proletariat and the founding of a new socialist society. Montessori decided to meet with these women and attempt to align them with all women's causes rather than having separate agendas for change. She believed it was the injustice to women that needed to be addressed and not their political affiliation.

She made an impassioned plea on the part of the propertied women, who were "abundantly represented" in the *Associazione Femminile*. These women had called upon Montessori "to initiate a mass protest against [a] scandalous injustice." She explained, "In Italy, and particularly in those provinces, which had earlier been a part of Austria, women had the right prior to unification, to independently administer the property, which they possessed. Today, after the unification, this right has been taken from them, even in the case where the woman lives in legal separation from her husband." She assailed the situation in which a husband can keep the woman subservient.[30]

Although Montessori did represent the propertied women's plight and called attention to the need for changes, she told the audience the following day that it was necessary to remember "those who helped to prepare through the labor of their hands our collective well-being and [those] who gave us the means to unite ourselves here in order to discuss our interests."[31] She was deeply concerned about the millions of women workers who had no voice at this congress. Her worry was that they were dominated not only by their husbands but also by their employers. She highlighted the distinct problems these women faced which she said were "made even more oppressive as a result of poverty." She urged the audience to become more conscious of the needs of the working woman. She appealed to their hearts and minds. "We are blind if we believe that the very same reforms are useful to them as they are to ourselves, and if we assume that they have, as do we, ample time to wait. It is an entirely different women's question," she contended, "which is united with our own."[32]

Mindful of the status of the women whom she was addressing, Montessori assured them that she was not departing from the theme of the women's movement to discuss socialist issues because it was not her intention to "speak about the wife of the worker, but the working woman." Conjecturing that the audience might believe that women should not work but should be home tending to their families, Montessori laid out a scenario in which the uneducated woman who knows nothing but subservience is forced by the existent law to earn a living when her husband can no longer provide for himself and the family. She recapitulated the law; "The wife has the obligation to help the husband and to contribute to his support." Then she offered her interpretation, "You should serve my pleasures when I can earn a living and work for me when I do not." She criticized the fact that when these women seek and find employment they are paid less than the man, and then proceeded to portray the life of this working wife graphically:

> She works like a man and consequently her domestic responsibilities do not cease. Instead of rest, which the husband requires after work, domestic chores await her and often yet with a child under her heart or at her breast. If the man seeks a diversion from his suffering in alcohol, then the woman becomes the recipient of the brutality of the drunkenness. Often too he would rather share

> his earnings with a less burdened female, rather than his own surrounded by children; for a smile he deprives his own of a piece of bread . . .[33]

Montessori's descriptions included abandonment, unfaithfulness on the wife's part because she is alone, need to support her family, prostitution by her daughters who do not want to live in poverty, and finally return of the jealously enraged husband who kills his wife. She implored, "Where are the laws which protect women in this predicament, in this position? Where is the law which declares the loss of rights for him who abandoned his family and remained away for years?"[34]

She was certainly not subtle in this speech. She needed to lay the groundwork for proposed legislation. She needed to ensure that women of means were able to empathize with the downtrodden working woman. She came well prepared with statistics and particulars and incisively presented them in her next two talks. Her major consideration was the fact that Italy had the largest number of working women among all the nations represented at the Congress and that generally speaking women earned barely half the wages paid to men.

Montessori was concerned about poor working conditions, to which everyone was exposed, but particularly women and children. She related in explicit detail the malformations affecting women and children from malodorous factory air and the deaths of many innocent children. "All of this," she said, "creates such a deep human and social agony that it moves even the heart of the wealthy and the lawmakers [who] have begun to afford the labor of women their protection."[35]

The new legislation for nursing mothers provided for them to remain at home for thirty days which led to a 5 % reduction in the mortality rate. She mocked the reality of the repercussions of these laws, "Men take pride, she said, "in the fact that they said to the little girl: Get rest for yourself! And to the mother of the newborns: Get rest for yourself!" How, she asked, can these women rest when they are hungry? They are forced despite their bodies' warnings to rest to" hurry back to the door of the workplace" rather than experience hunger.[36]

No one seems to have escaped Montessori's rancor. She railed against employers, doctors, scientists and the wealthy. She censured the actions of both the Congregazione di Carita (the congress of charity) in Rome which she maintained was "wealthy and restricted to the protection of only loyal Catholics, lets a poor mother who is needy repeatedly climb up and down the stairs before they will approve her monthly pension of 3.50 Lira," and Rome's *'Komitee Soccorso e Lavoro'* "which consists of ladies of the courtly society, [who] provide on the basis of need, work for only very few women;" Neither of these groups of "privileged ladies" she contended, allocated enough to provide adequate nutrition for a mother and her children. Work, she contended, was preferable to donations, but wage equality was necessary to make this option worthwhile. This responsibility she lay at the door of her audience.[37]

She charged them to take action. "The commerce, which exploits female patience," she declared, "is one of the most criminal aspects which exist in modern society." She protested, "I demand the liberation of these oppressed women! with all my strength I insist that the principle of justice be universally supported: 'for equal work, equal wages.'" She concluded with a motion for equal pay for women to those of male workers."[38] This motion was enthusiastically and unanimously accepted.

Newspapers both in Germany and all over Europe covered this first International Women's Congress. Many of them concentrated on the style of presentation and the beauty of the speaker instead of on the words which Montessori shared with the women in Berlin. Some carried a photograph of Montessori, which was widely published and described "the distinguished lady in the accompanying photograph [as] lovely looking—dark eyes, a Mona Lisa smile, a frilled collar, and a strand of pearls setting off the face framed with soft curls."[39]

Annoyed by the admiration of her person expressed in the newspapers, Montessori wrote a letter to her parents after the congress. She promised, "My picture will never again appear in newspapers and nobody will again dare to poetize my supposed charms. I shall do serious work.[40]

Maria Montessori had already begun to do "serious work" but the outside world at the end of the nineteenth century did not take women's work seriously. She would become one of the women who would help change this mindset. Her participation at the Congress gave her close contact with the culture and politics of European women while the media attention brought a greater awareness of the power of the media, which she would draw upon later in her career.

The decade in which Montessori was in medical school was an exciting one in the growth of ideas about and the recognition of the importance of childhood. The fields of anthropology, hygiene, and pedagogy were being researched all over Europe and the United States. Education became the new word of the times. It was seen as a method of strengthening the body and the mind of those individuals of tomorrow. Later, Montessori would call this period, "The Discovery of Childhood."

Although Italy was behind countries such as France, England and Germany in its scientific research and establishment of institutions for individuals with mental challenges, by the 1880s it too had begun to explore the problems of the care and education of these children. The initiative for this movement can be credited to the awareness of the major impact science could play in society. Montessori's professors such as Bonfigli, Santa de Sanctis, and Labriola had introduced this topic into their lectures. Her intellect was piqued by the many possibilities for intervention.

In 1898, the first Italian Pedagogical Congress was held in Turin. About 3000 educators participated at this Congress. Maria Montessori was one of the participants and speakers. Although she said she felt like an intruder because the "happy marriage" of medicine and pedagogy had not yet taken place, she approached it with a new passion, a new mission and transformation of a newly recognized class, the class of educators. She attended the conference with a specific plan to convince educators to join this new union between education and medicine, to look to science for new answers to old questions about children with mental disabilities.

At this Congress, she argued for separate institutions for children with mental deficiencies, which would enable them to become productive citizens and for special courses for teachers designed to enable them to teach these youngsters. She closed her speech with the challenging reproach that anyone who failed to support her vision [did not have] "the right to be called a civilized person in this day and age; this is not sentiment or rhetoric," she said, "but sanity and science."[41]

As we look at the advances in education for children with disabilities today, this first step by Montessori over one hundred years ago may seem insignificant and perhaps even unjust in isolating these children, but we must remember there was no education at all for children with disabilities at the time.

Babini raised the question as to why Montessori was nominated as the delegate to go to Turin to represent the doctors at this Pedagogical Congress. She examined some possibilities. It was her belief that first Montessori had earned the right by working as diligently as the nominal secretary for the formation of the National League for the Education and Care of the Mentally Retarded. This League would not be formally constituted until January 1899, six months after the Turin Congress, but was already in its preliminary stage. The fact that Montessori was a woman and had proven skills in persuasive argument and might be perceived at the Congress as less authoritarian, less intrusive and less dangerous than a male all seemed to work in favor of her nomination. She was also seen as a competent clinical psychiatrist who was constantly in search of new support for an initiative in favor of children with mental challenges.

One of her supporters was her Professor, Professor Bonfigli who had been elected to Parliament two years earlier and had been one of the founding members of the soon to be established League. Although he was an authority in the scientific and professional field, he had not published any works on the issue of children with disabilities. Montessori, on the other hand, had published an article on the subject entitled, "Social Poverty and the New Discoveries in Science." She had pointed out the hard work in the field by Professor Bonfigli, but, according to Babini she had also made it clear "it was she at this particular moment who was most informed to talk about what was being done in Europe and what would, could and should have happened in Italy in the field of education."[42]

During the time Montessori worked with Giuseppe Montesano on behalf of children with educational challenges she also traveled to Paris. There, she observed the Bourneville Institute, which worked with children with mental retardation. She also studied the work of Seguin and Itard, both of whom worked with children with special needs. Still further, Montessori was supported by the wives of influential politicians in Rome who had also been active in the fields of social, health and medical assistance to women and children. For all these reasons it seems she was most qualified to speak at this conference.

While this Congress was in session, Queen Elizabeth of Austria was slain. Montessori used this event to emphasize the need for immediate changes in the social fabric of society, pointing out that the weak individuals of today could possibly become the alienated and antisocial of tomorrow. Her ideas were well received at the Congress. The attendees approved, by acclamation, her proposal to introduce special needs classrooms to house children with degenerative conditions. A Roman newspaper commented after the successful speech, "this redemption of the individual happens at the hand of a highly humanitarian work of intellect and compassion. It is obvious that a woman would be behind it."[43]

This was the only the beginning of many years of speeches and articles on behalf of women, children, and children with disabilities. Her most vocal backing came from the Minister for Public Education, Baccelli. On December 22, 1898, a few short months after the Turin Congress, he invited her to lecture in three teacher training schools in Rome. He was extremely instrumental in encouraging all school boards to follow the lead of the League for the Education of the Mentally Retarded in providing education and schooling for children with mental challenges. The inaugural course at the teacher training schools, as reported by the Roman newspapers, referred to the "incredible competence and assuredness of the young scientist who touches on themes that are incredibly relevant for the social aspects of the country and broaches on arguments and issues that are more or less ignored in Italy."[44]

That same year, 1899, under the auspices of the National League for the Education and Care of the Mentally Retarded, with the proceeds going to a public kitchen to feed the sick and poor and a shelter for the indigent, Montessori presented a lecture in four Italian cities entitled, "The New Woman." She charged her audiences, which included most of the prominent women of the communities, with the task of pursuing scientific reasoning. "Women themselves must enter the field of positive science," she said, "must argue with their brains not their hearts. Women…Have to confront men, to debate with them, to work alongside them, to join them in discovering the truth."[45]

This emphasis on economic independence and the use of women's intellectual powers, a premise Montessori would highlight time and time again, is known as scientific feminism. Babini wrote, "Her scientific feminism was one of the most original tiles of a large mosaic which was Italian feminism . . . [It was] not the only one that Maria Montessori would bring to the feminist cause. Without a doubt it also had very deep roots and also painful ones in her personal and professional life."[46]

Scientific feminism would remain a theme of Montessori's for many years to come. More than twenty years later, at a course in England, Montessori recalled a story from one of the scientific conferences she had attended in Vienna. To prove a point she reminisced about a woman who stood up at a conference where the scientists had proven conclusively the incompatibility of working with the brain and the functions of motherhood. "My friends and colleagues, said the woman scientist, please disprove my nine children."[47]

One of the highlights during these years of activism was Montessori's presence at the International Feminist Congress in London in 1899. Its main goal was to organize existent women's activities in the world, to demonstrate how much they had already accomplished and to make public how much more they intended to achieve. Montessori's attendance was funded partially by the National League for the Education and Care of the Mentally Retarded and its President Giuseppe Montesano and partially by minister Baccelli, who sent her the money directly while she was conducting research in Paris and attending the meeting of the National Association for Promoting the Welfare of the Feeble-minded. She was the only Italian representative and delegate at this London conference. She took the podium three times, once to welcome the Italian participants, then to speak of the rural teachers and their newly constituted maternal union for the protection of elementary school teachers and lastly to speak about a proposed law in Italy to prohibit children under fourteen from working in sulfur mines and to solicit backing from the English government towards this end.

Bringing the message of scientific and practical feminism to improve the life of women and children in Italy was the life she led in the years ending the nineteenth century and beginning the new century. Some of the innovations that she and the philanthropic women of Rome achieved for women and children were sanitariums for women with tuberculosis, colonies in the

Apennines for convalescing children, laboratories for poor mothers, centers for abandoned children, and institutions and separate classrooms for children with mental disabilities. Montessori clearly continued to express a feminist position in public orally and in print, taking advantage of her innate persuasive abilities and the power of the press, which she inspired. Her lectures throughout Italy and Europe became commonplace occurrences.

Montessori continued her hospital work, her medical practice, and her endeavors on behalf of the National League for the Education of Retarded Children. Additionally, in 1899, she accepted an appointment as a Lecturer in Hygiene and Anthropology at the *Reggio Istituto Superiore di Magistero Femminile*, a teacher-training college for women. This experience provided her with knowledge of pedagogical curriculum and an understanding of the history and methodology of education. It enabled her also to make contacts with faculty and students in education.

One year later, 1n 1900, when the League opened an institute to train teachers in the education of children with mental deficiencies with an on-site demonstration school, Montessori, who had urged the founding of such an institution, was appointed its co-director with Giuseppe Montesano who was now the chief physician of the mental asylum in Rome. Montessori explored Wundt's scientific method of observation, Sergi's research in anthropological studies, and the work of Seguin and Itard on children with special needs. She prepared a scientific environment to observe and "discover the child."[48] Experiencing success with these teachers and children, Montessori pursued further formal studies at the University of Rome in pedagogical studies.

In 1901, she left the Orthophrenic School (training institute), apparently for personal reasons, (the marriage of Montesano, her co-director and father of her child, to Maria Aprile). The end of this relationship did not deter her from carrying on her radical agenda. One chapter in her life had come to an end, but she continued writing and lecturing to advance the causes of women and children.

In 1881, when Montessori was only eleven years old, Anna Maria Mozzoni founded the first Italian women's association, the Lega per la Promozione degli Interessi Femminili (League for the Promotion of Women's Interests), in Milan. Its goal was to raise the consciousness of all women and to direct their efforts to the social needs of women in society.

Anna Maria Mozzoni was born in Milan, Italy in 1837. By the time she was eighteen years old she had published a play in French. Several years later her interests turned to the need for women's emancipation. She became a prolific writer, publishing many articles on the subject.

Before women began to organize into their own special interest groups, the campaign for women's freedom had been sustained mainly by well-to-do women who were involved in hands-on projects on behalf of poor and working class women. Women's needs and how best to approach the issues varied greatly. Some women believed in the "concept of equality between men and women and interpreted the rights of all citizens as 'neuter'- that is, not connoted by gender." Others sought to obtain complete legal and social parity. They argued for the equivalence of men and women, stressing the "distinctive values of female experience and identity. "This latter group, composed of greater numbers of women than the former, emerged into a group of women who embraced social feminism."[49]

Many feminists in the 1890s, Montessori among them, also favored social feminism. Bortolotti, an Italian feminist historian, asserted that "this political movement was one of the most highly developed of the democratic feminist movements of that period, and sought to develop ties with other such movements throughout the world." She cited many international connections, including Mozzoni's role in the First International Congress for the Rights of Women held in Paris in 1878. The political agenda for the program she contended was largely supplied for them by John Stuart Mill, whose work on *The Subjection of Women* was translated into Italian by Anna Mozzoni in 1870, the year of Montessori's birth. Bortolotti wrote that the ballot, freedom from male domination, and access to non-domestic jobs were all linked together as the basis for the emancipation movement. She stressed its "concern for social equality and personal liberty."[50] This theme would later be incorporated into many of Montessori's speeches.

Although no direct link between Montessori and Mozzoni has been made before 1906, when they jointly petitioned the Italian government of various cities for the vote for women, it is evident Montessori was attuned to the tenets of social feminism and most likely knew Mozzoni and her work much before that date. Not only did Montessori speak to the Socialist women who were protesting at the Women's International Congress in Berlin in 1896 and echo the sentiments of the social feminists in all of her talks at that conference and future conferences, but her life choices clearly reflect these beliefs.

On May 18, 1902, Montessori gave an address in Rome on the future of women .In it she chararacterized the feminist movement in the modern world as one that was advancing with incredible speed and could not be stopped.[51]

Her participation in the suffragist movement, however, appears to have run its course. In 1906, shortly before the opening of the first Casa dei Bambini, she petitioned for the vote with Mozzoni but at another conference held in the same year she was silent on the debate on women's right to vote, which centered around the ability or inability of women to take care of their children if they were to become involved in the world of politics. She had addressed this issue in 1902, claiming that the education of children was becoming a collective work and should be the mission of the state. In an article in *La Vita* in May 1907, she expressed a deep dissatisfaction with the world of politics.[52] She had already moved into another chapter in her life, leaving behind the world of medicine and politics.

Her work with the children from the Orthophrenic School and the system of education that she developed during this experience came to the attention of Eduardo Talamo through the Mayor of Rome, Ernesto Nathan, whose wife was a supporter of Montessori. Talamo was praised as "an engineer of unusual ability and a philanthropist of the highest order."[53] He built a housing complex in the San Lorenzo district of Rome for the poor. Talamo believed regardless of the class a person came from the family should have a clean and comfortable home, that all children should be able to live carefree lives during their formative years and should be taught by an encouraging and guiding teacher.

Talamo's new tenements housed as many as fifty children between the ages of three and seven who were not yet attending public schools. In an effort to protect his property and in keeping with his beliefs on the developmental importance of these years, Talamo offered Montessori a position in his buildings, which would provide the first full-day childcare in the nation. She accepted, assuming the position of Director of what would become known as the Casa dei Bambini (Children's House). It would become the first of many.

At the inauguration of the second Casa, Montessori proclaimed, "Today the social and economic evolution calls the working-woman to take her place among the wage-earners, . . . The mother must, in any event, leave her child, and often with the pain of knowing him to be abandoned. . . . We can no longer say that the convenience of leaving their children takes away from the mother a natural social duty of first importance: namely, that of caring for and educating her tender offspring."[54]

The language of this statement echoes the sentiments Montessori had expressed publicly for over ten years. She had become a different woman than she had been prior to her experiences in medical school and on the talk-circuit in countries all over Europe. Almost one hundred years later, her statement still resonates with working women as strongly as when she made it.

Maria Montessori declared, "We are communizing… A 'maternal function,' a feminine duty within the house. … The home will be transformed and will assume the functions of the woman. I believe that in the future of society other forms of communistic life will come."[55] Here we see a continuation of her beliefs in social feminism.

She proposed a "house infirmary" for sick children to enable the working mother to continue working. This infirmary would also serve to isolate the child from the rest of the children in the family, thus preventing contagion. Further, she advanced the notion of a communal kitchen with the food served by a dumb-waiter to each family's dining room in the evening after a long day's work. She envisioned the tenements as "centres (Br.) of education, of refinement, of comfort" with clubs and reading rooms for the men. The latter she predicted, would help to close gambling houses and saloons. Her ideas presaged past and current debates, mainly by women, of what she termed, "the union of the family and the school in the matter of educational aims." She raised the issue of the parents' right to visit the school at any time. At her schools, she authorized "mothers . . . [to] go at any hour of the day to watch, to admire, or to meditate upon the life there."

She counseled the celebrants that not only was there not to be a dissolution of the home and family brought on by the changing social and economic conditions that forced women to work but, "The home itself assumes the gentle feminine attributes of the domestic housewife."[56]

Still maintaining egalitarian notions that she had espoused previously, Montessori was proud of the fact that the women of these refurbished tenements could say, in the same manner rich women said, "I have left my son with the governess and the nurse, the house physician watches over [my children] and directs their sane and sturdy growth."[57]

Both men and women were to share in the comforts of the new home that Montessori detailed, but the women, she declared, "would be liberated from all those attributes which once made [them] desirable to man only as the source of the maternal blessings of existence. She shall be, like man, an individual, a free human being who like man would be entitled to the same comforts of the communized home."[58]

Pearl Boggs observed, "In studying Montessori's writings with the utmost care it occurred to me that the chief cause of [her] uniqueness is that she has thought and wrought as a thorough woman. A carefully trained scientist, she has interpreted scientific facts from a woman's viewpoint. A conscientious student of humanity and its needs she finds a woman's solution for its betterment."[59]

She delineated the elements of the woman's viewpoint to include cherishing, nurturing activities, immediate ends, sure results, individualism, and independence. Boggs interpreted Montessori's views as feminine. She speculated that if Montessori schools were to become more popular, "We shall find feminine ideals in the schools where today masculine ones prevail."[60]

Montessori herself, when asked if she were a feminist on her first trip to America in 1912, would not use the "F" word" to interpret her work. She said she thought of it as an effort to elevate the status of women and to bring freedom or liberty to all children. Montessori's view of freedom or liberty for all children was in direct opposition to the prevailing thought of the time which viewed children as miniature adults who warranted continual monitoring by adults, to be confined to stationary desks and chairs and to recite teacher-directed curriculum in unison. For Montessori, liberty was the aim of all education. Liberty is activity she contended, and discipline comes through liberty. Children are disciplined when they are "master[s] of [themselves] and can, therefore, regulate [their] own conduct."[61] She regarded the child as capable of acquiring from the environment as much as it systematically offered him or her.

Montessori, unlike many women and men today, always used masculine adjectives and nouns to describe children and other people in her writings. However, her intent is evident to writers of both sexes. In selecting Montessori for his book entitled, *Woman as Revolutionary*, Frederick C. Griffin underscored this fact: "the emphasis of the volume is on women whose efforts were not confined to increasing the rights and opportunities of their sex, but rather, were devoted primarily to the exaltation of the human spirit common to both sexes."[62] On her arrival in New York City in 1913, in response to reporters' questions about suffrage, Montessori claimed not to be a militant, but said, "Anything that broadens the race and broadens the individuals must be approved."[63] This statement was a turn-about from the radical stand she and Anna Marie Mozzoni had taken only six years before.

One year later, however, in May 1914, she attended a Women's Congress held in Rome. *The New York Times* characterized this Congress which was held every five years as "Woman's Week," in which resolutions were passed and plans determined for the next five years. In addition to business there were many social events taking place, each attempting to outdo the others. One of these parties was held by Maria Montessori for the American delegates to reciprocate for the hospitality she had received in the United States during her prior lecture tour. The Congress was attended by Queen Elene of Italy who dubbed her eldest daughter (then twelve years old) a democrat and a feminist who believed that all people were equal and said that if her daughter carried through with these beliefs the women's movement would go very far in Italy.[64]

In actuality, Montessori continued to place her hopes for the future with women. In London a few years later, she said "the future progress of the world lies in the hands of woman—[sic] that her hope lies in woman [sic]—that the utilization of her discoveries rests entirely with the mothers and the teachers of the world."[65]

She consciously developed her method and her aspirations for a peaceable world with children of both sexes at its core. "If we wish to alter the habits and customs of a country, Montessori wrote, "or if we wish to accentuate more vigorously the characteristics of a people, we must take as our instrument the child."[66] Throughout most of her life, the belief that her method of education held the potential for peaceable change was uppermost in her mind. This view was carried through to her death. This sentiment can even be found on her headstone, "I beg the all-powerful children to unite with me for the building of peace in man and in the world."[67]

Because of this goal for her method, she was always quite concerned that it had been bastardized in many countries around the world as well as in her native Italy where it had also been modified or entirely neglected. She worried about its absence from her country. While Montessori claimed that her method had been besmirched by some, others in Italy continued to uphold her method and to raise funds for the greater diffusion of her educational reform. On June 26, 1918 *La Societa Amici del Metodo Montessori* (The Society of Friends of the Montessori Method) was formed in Naples.

In 1919, during a visit to Italy, Montessori had an audience with the Pope. He directed that her books be included in the Vatican library. At approximately the same time, she was promised by the Italian Under-Secretary for Home Affairs he would try to have the Montessori system adopted throughout Italy. Naples planned to transform twenty schools to her method immediately.[68] This plan would enable her to realize her dream of reintroduction of her method in Italy in the manner she envisioned it.

On April 4, 1922, shortly before Mussolini took over the Italian government, Antonino Anile, the Italian Minister of Education approached Montessori, who was then visiting Rome from Barcelona. He told her the Municipality of Rome had adopted her method in numerous elementary and nursery schools for which he was financially responsible. He appointed her formally Inspector of these schools. About seven weeks later he extended her inspectorate appointment to all of Italy and she was asked to conduct teacher training courses there.[69] Montessori welcomed this appointment and a chance to reintroduce an unadulterated version of her method to Italy. She left her home in Spain and moved back to Italy.

In a letter to the editor Montessori praised Anile as a "name of repute in the world of medicine, and a man of keen and ardent mind, in touch with the problems of the world about him." She wrote that he had just delivered in the Chamber a "brilliant speech, which will mark an epoch in the annals of our legislation." In this talk he maintained, "To care for our youngest children was an indispensable measure in the eyes of anyone who believed that social life has its roots in the life of the individual. . . . In the early years of childhood lies the secret of racial and human betterment."[70]

The philosophies of Montessori and Anile were certainly parallel to each other. Shortly after Mussolini took over the government, however, he appointed the distinguished Italian philosopher, Giovanni Gentile, Minister of Education as a means of obtaining respectability with the nation's intellectuals. Gentile, too, was very supportive of Montessori education and the Society of Friends of the Montessori Method. His beliefs encompassed the idea that, "since the nature of spirit is movement and perpetual creation, every teacher and pupil are something new in comparison with all others."[71] This philosophy seemed to dovetail with Montessori's beliefs as did the mandated textbook utilized by the elementary classroom teachers, Lombardo-Radice's *Lezione di didattica* (Teaching Lessons). It included the following ideas: "The teacher must engage the child's interest with a wide range of activities but always leading to development—that is, to the life of the mind. A method is good if it pushes the child to think and to work; a lesson is good if it becomes a personal conquest of knowledge on the part of the child; techniques are good if they arise out of the organic character of the work; discipline is good if it is demanded by the work and not mere passive obedience."[72]

Many of these ideas from Lombardo Radice's 1913 book could have been taken from the pages of Montessori's, *Scientific Pedagogy as Applied to Child Education in the Children's Houses*, which was written in fifteen days,[73] and published in Italy in 1909 (later translated in 1912 into English as *The Montessori Method*). It is no wonder that she was so accepting of the idea of spreading her method of early education throughout Italy.

In practice, however, the schools were teacher-centered rather than child-centered. The "Fascist Doctrine as Presented Officially by Mussolini," (June 1932) states, "The Fascist conception of life stresses the importance of the State and accepts the individual only in so far as his interests coincide with those of the State."[74] The first part of this document was written by Gentile.

One wonders what Gentile's motives in supporting Montessori were as it is evident he did not believe in individuality. Shortly after taking office he eliminated the teaching of pedagogy in the new teacher training schools and did away with student teaching. Instead these newly formed teacher training schools which replaced the old substandard normal schools emphasized Latin and philosophy.

Some of the features of the Gentile reforms during his two years as Minister of Education are noteworthy. His reforms of 1923 set up a number of tracks in the Italian educational system which effectively deprived many students of higher education; his reforms de-emphasized both technical education and foreign languages. Instead, history, art, religion, and other elements of national culture were stressed. To "use the slogan of the Gentile reformers, the school was to be formative rather than informative."[75] There was also a deliberate attempt to impede the progress of female students. His reforms also made religious instruction in Catholic doctrine mandatory in the lower grades of all state schools. His goal was fewer schools but good ones.

The focal point of his reforms, commonly called the Gentile reforms, was the classical high school for which students had to take rigid State examinations. These examinations were open to the students in the Catholic primary and secondary schools, giving them the capability of competing with the State schools, for the first time. The accord between Church and State was tenuous at best. Both Mussolini and the Church sought the same goal: the hearts and minds of Italy's youth.

Mussolini soon discovered these entrance examinations were blocking the efforts of the lower middle classes' aspirations to further their children through the educational system. Feeling the pressure from this group, he began to withdraw his support for Gentile's reforms as early as 1924. Gentile, however, "remained loyal to Mussolini until his own death at the hands of the resistance partisans in April 1944." Tannenbaum commenting on this devout loyalty wrote, "Even Bottai, the most influential Fascist with any brains throughout the history of the regime, turned again the Duce before that."[76]

Education was never stable in Italy during the Fascist period. There were eight ministers of education from 1922–1936. Noted historian Dennis Mack Smith described the state of education: "the syllabus and curriculum for schools were repeatedly changed; textbooks were rewritten when Fedele wanted more religion, or when Ercole wanted more economics, and yet more radically when de Vecchi ordained that every detail of education must be infused with the highest fascist principles."[77]

Montessori seemed to be comfortable with her additional responsibilities in Italy, and continued her educational activities there and in other countries as she had done before the Fascist takeover of Italy. During most of this period she continued to supervise teachers for her schools and train new teachers for the existent Montessori schools not only in Italy, but also in Spain, and England.

Mussolini, nevertheless, seemed unsure of the advantage of Montessori to his regime. Therefore, in 1924, the Italian government undertook an inquiry into the recognition and acceptance of Montessori education in foreign countries all over the world. By early 1924, after Mussolini read the research he declared that in the English cities they could see only two Italian things: Marconi's telegraph and Montessori's method. The results were of a magnitude which surprised even the Ministry which had conducted the study. It is reported that when Mussolini saw these results he pronounced," . . . the Montessori principle is established and those who fail to understand it 'display their own ignorance.'"[78] Schwegman reported that "he launched himself as the Italian savior of her method that risked being lost throughout Italy."[79]

On June 17, 1923 the *Ente Morale* officially became a corporation. By April 8, 1924, perhaps motivated by Montessori's return to Italy and Mussolini's survey, the society name was changed to Ente Morale Opera Montessori (Incorporated Society for the Works of Montessori) and its headquarters moved to its permanent home in Rome.[80]

Mussolini asked his then Minister of Education, Gentile, to initiate a six-month Montessori teacher training course conducted by Dr. Montessori in Milan. There were one hundred fifty participants with sixty of them having been sent by the government. Mussolini was the honorary president of the course.

In 1926, he assumed the presidency of the Montessori Society and continued to offer it substantial support. His Ministers of Education and of the Colonies were joint vice-presidents of the society. Distinguished Italian Princes and other dignitaries became members of the Honorary Committee. A monthly publication entitled, *L'Idea Montessori* publicized the Montessori movement in Italy and throughout the world. In the first issue, Montessori asserted the child's right "to grow to full stature, spiritual[ly] and physical[ly] . . . not hindered by the grown-ups."[81] Montessori's words seemed to be prophetic.

The "grown-ups" had a completely different agenda for the youth of Italy. Other individuals and nations saw the potential for educating the child to fulfill the needs of their societies. Montessori elucidated this position, "the implications of this theory are very far reaching. It was by acting on children that the totalitarian governments were able to build up huge reserves of young fanatics, devoted to their leader and filled with warlike spirit.[82]

The program of Il Duce was to control the child both spiritually and physically. Indoctrination began at a very early age. The campaign for children's minds was extended beyond the school and the Church. In 1926, the regime established the Opera Nazionale Balilla which was responsible for the political and physical education of elementary school children. Physical fitness became a major part of the training and Mussolini had arenas built for the display of the physical and military prowess of Italy's youth.

Troops of children were formed by age six (Balilla). "Mounted and helmeted, [they] paraded in uniform before Il Duce. As they grew older they moved on to other organizations; Balilla Escursionisti (campers—aged eight to twelve), Balilla Moschettieri (musketeers—aged twelve to fourteen), Avanguardisti moschietierri (fourteen to sixteen) and Avanguardisti mitraglieri (machine-gunners—sixteen to eighteen).Every year a convocation was held in Mussolini's forum near Rome featuring these organizations. Songs and hymns extolling the virtues of Il Duce played an important part in the training of these groups.[83]

In addition to the spiritual and physical transformation of older Italian children, in the early years of his regime, Mussolini was intent upon transforming the entire educational system in order to create a new fascist citizen. He envisioned children as young as six years old wearing military-like uniforms, giving the fascist salute and singing fascist songs in all of the schools. Would he seek the minds of even younger children? This was foreshadowed when three months after the signing of the Lateran Treaty (1929) between Church and State Mussolini claimed the right of Fascism to educate all of the children of Italy. "'Book and Musket, the perfect Fascist,' was his mobilization order to the country's cradles, for even in kindergarten a six-year old Son of the Wolf, as toddlers were known, was being prepared for the day eight years later when he would don the Fascist black shirt and drill with a musket."[84] By 1934 Mussolini wanted to make these same regulations applicable to all nursery schools including Montessori's schools for children from three to five years of age.

By the later 1930's, Tannenbaum wrote, "the youth organizations impinged increasingly on school life, so that it is almost impossible to separate the impact of the two on teachers and children alike."[85] Montessori began to see the impending signs of major changes.

Obviously, not everyone agreed with the policies which were being instituted during and after school. School teachers, nonetheless, were asked to swear an oath to fascism early in the regime. Teachers who either overtly spoke against the government or were suspected of disloyalty were dismissed, mainly secondary teachers. In 1931, university professors also were required to take an oath. Smith claimed that the Minister of Education privately reassured them that it was just a formality and they would not be required to conform. The appearance of university support of the government by outsiders was important to the regime and less than one percent of the university faculty failed to take the oath. After initial acquiescence, these same professors were asked to join the party and swear an additional oath to "live or die" for Mussolini. "Teaching could no longer be neutral;" wrote Smith, "it had to be fascist and justify the new ethic of violence, obedience, and intellectual uniformity. Most intellectuals in positions of authority kept their jobs."[86] For a long time Montessori kept hers.

Personally, Mussolini was not opposed to women in his regime. More accurately speaking, Mussolini was not opposed to women in his bed during his regime. Gallo alleged that Mussolini found time for women in his very busy daily schedule, and claimed, "Navarra said that Il Duce had a new woman every day in Palazza Venezia." He then commented, "Of course Navarra was exaggerating, but the reality was populated enough."[87] In spite of his proclivities for women, Mussolini was convinced that "in our state the woman should not matter."[88]

Montessori unquestionably would not have agreed with that statement. Her early career decision, her willingness to defy the conventional standards of her time, and her public addresses urging women to join men in seeking the truth are indicative of her belief in the importance of women and their freedom and independence.

Her stance was not in keeping with the defined gender roles of the fascist regime. Women's emancipation of any sort was opposed. They were encouraged to make sacrifices for their country by staying at home and having children. Paid employment outside the home was denounced early in the 1920s and as unemployment became more prevalent throughout Italy this crusade became even more fervent. "For women," Mussolini asserted, "work was potentially dangerous and might make them sterile, whereas for men it was a source of 'great physical and moral virility.'"[89] Laws advancing these positions were introduced. Abortion, contraception, and even information on contraception were banned. Many incentives for marriage and family were offered, coupled with disincentives for bachelors and childless couples.

This emphasis on motherhood was not a novel course in Italy. The Fascist years were part of an historical continuum reflecting traditional Italian views on women's place in the political, economic, and social structure of Italian society. Women were viewed in the same manner by both Church and State. Where they differed, wrote Perry, was that "Mussolini [placed stress] on the imperialist role of the 'prolific mothers,' whereas the Church's primary concern was with preserving the 'virtue' and 'respectability' of women who might be tainted by contact with the outside world."[90]

Either faction would have looked askance at Montessori. She had originally chosen to work in a field which was virtually all male. Her outside contact, both literally and figuratively, resulted in a child at the turn of the twentieth century when she was an unmarried mother; certainly not in keeping with the Church's design for women.

Her views on peace and peace education were in direct opposition to Mussolini's call to raise one's child for militaristic sacrifice. For Montessori peace was not just an absence of war. She held an intense belief in the goodness of the individual child and educating him/her to change the world to a peaceable place. Mussolini saw the same potential for educating the child to fulfill the needs of the fascist society. Their views were in direct conflict to each other. No one could remain neutral under this regime.

Many discussions began to appear in culturally liberal magazines in the mid-1930s questioning the ideas of the time. Although strictly speaking they were not magazines of political opposition, their contributions were certainly not insignificant. "Around these magazines gathered the best of liberal culture that refused to bow down and become regimented." Among the many notable liberals listed were "Keynes and Maria Montessori (with her appeal for peace education) and many other authors who could not easily fit the fascist perspective."[91] Montessori's appeals for peace education were in direct opposition to the military build-up so evident in Mussolini's programs. Her entire demeanor was in direct opposition to government policies.

Rita Kramer claimed that friction already had begun to surface between Montessori and the Italian leadership when the new policies directed at young children were initiated. Montessori, she reported, fled to Spain, refusing to work any longer under the Mussolini regime. Schwegman narrowed the breakdown to a specific international Montessori conference in April 1934 when Montessori was speaking about her method and peace. Montessori alleged that fascist surveillance was present at this conference. While she was speaking they all heard whistles. Maria sent Mario to find out what was happening. When he returned to report she immediately ended the conference and left the country.[92]

Francesca Claremont, a devoted English follower of Montessori, gave me another account of Montessori's flight from Italy. She claimed that she and Montessori went to Mussolini's office to discuss whether or not Montessori would permit the children in her schools to wear these uniforms and participate in these ceremonies. Claremont alleged that Mussolini kept lion cubs chained to the end of his desk. Montessori, she asserted, told Mussolini that she believed in democracy and would not allow these rituals in her schools. In spite of lion cubs. I spent more than twenty- five years chasing those lions down.

In pursuit of these lions, I read or skimmed almost every biography written about Mussolini, I wrote to the mayor of Predappio, the town where he was born. The mayor sent me a picture of Mussolini with lion cubs at a zoo, one which I already possessed. But, then I found the same picture in a biography with the caption "Mussolini and *his* lion cubs." After lots of reading I finally tracked down three biographies that mention Mussolini and lions. Roy MacGregor-Hastie in his biography, *The Day of the Lion: The Life and Death of Fascist Italy, 1922–1945* (the title refers to the fact that Mussolini was born under the astrological sign of Leo) wrote, "on July 27th [1923] an admirer gave the Duce a lion cub, which he insisted on keeping in his drawing room. He would sniff as he entered the room and say to his guests: 'Ah! A smell of lion here!"[93]

In Richard Collier's biography, *Duce: a Biography of Benito Mussolini*, the number of lions increases four-fold. He explained, "Wild animals still fascinated [Mussolini] . . . And pets on the household roster included a royal eagle, a falcon, a monkey, two gazelles, two tortoises, and Pippo, the ginger angora cat. For two months father and sons enjoyed a daily gambol with four lion cubs housed on the verandah until [his wife], past patience, packed them off to the zoo."[94] Collier makes another reference to Mussolini's fascination with lions. He writes of Il Duce's desire "to make a mark on my era . . . like a lion with its claw." He then, according to Collier, proceeded to demonstrate by scraping his nails down the back of a leather chair.[95]

Laura Fermi, too, makes mention of the lions in Mussolini's life. She referred to a book by his son Vittorio in which he recollects a huge white porcelain eagle placed on the grand piano in the living room with a live puma bound to its leg. The puma had been a gift from an Argentinean admirer and when it got larger and fiercer it was sent to the zoo. There was also a lioness named, "Italia," which was allowed to roam the apartment, but also was eventually shipped to the zoo and visited by Mussolini. "When the lioness was still a cub, he used to take her riding in his open Alfa Romeo along the wooded avenues of the Villa Borghese, so that the strollers in the park would see the daring man and his pet and talk of them to others."[96] These stories lend considerable credence to substantiate Claremont's contention. I would like to think that this scene really transpired. In spite of lion cubs!

Montessori's firm conviction of freedom and peace for the child enabled her to take an uncompromising stand against these proposed policies for all schools in Italy. Within one day of her refusal to adopt these regulations and her departure for Spain, all of her schools were officially closed in Italy.

In Germany and Austria, which were under Nazi rule, circumstances were even more extreme; not only were Montessori's schools closed in both countries, but an effigy of Montessori was burned over a pyre of her own books in a public square both in Berlin and Vienna.

Rita Kramer devoted considerable space in her biography of Montessori demonstrating that Montessori worked closely with the fascist government in spite of being aware of their "daily increment of observable repression and brutality."[97] Marjan Schwegman in a book entitled *Maria Montessori*, written in Dutch and translated into Italian uses much of Kramer's research for her chapter entitled, "Maria, the Catholics and Mussolini: The Separation from Italy," but she is less harsh in her judgment of Montessori's decision to return to Italy to reintroduce her method, which had become adulterated after she and her son left Italy in 1916 to make their home in Barcelona.

Contrary to Rita Kramer's indictment that Montessori was aware of the brutality and oppression in Mussolini's Italy, I believe that Montessori's desire to implant her unmodified method and her original schools firmly in her native land, her staunch conviction in the universality of her method to promote peace and her belief that her ideas were apolitical, enabled her to continue to promote her schools and her teacher training in Italy while Mussolini was in power.

Maria Jervolino, the former President of the "Opera Montessori" reinforced my conviction. She wrote, "When social decadence has gradually or suddenly threatened the liberty of a people, without fail Montessori schools have been opposed or closed."[98]

Montessori asserted all children were culture free. She affirmed that education must be super-civic. She claimed to be apolitical. She resolutely held to this idea. In 1947, in a letter sent to all governments, she proclaimed, "no child is a Bolshevist or a fascist or a democrat; they all become what circumstances or the environment make them."[99]

Conflict seemed to follow Montessori. When she fled back to Spain, where she had previously set up schools in Barcelona associated with the Catholic Church, the Spanish Civil War erupted. Once again her life and property were in danger. She fled once again; this time to the Netherlands. Three years later she was invited to India by the Theosophical Society to give a course in Adyar-Madras. After Italy joined World War II, she was interned to their compound as an Italian national. Her son Mario was confined in a camp in Amednagar. On her seventieth birthday she received a telegram from the Viceroy of India which read, "We have long thought what to give you for your 70th birthday. We thought the best present we could give you, was to send you back your son."[100] It seems all of the talk of Mario as her nephew or adopted son no longer mattered to a more enlightened society. She continued to offer courses in India where her method spread rapidly.

All of these obstacles do not appear to have altered Montessori's beliefs or drive. She returned to Europe after the Second World War and continued to espouse her tenet that, "to change a generation or nation, to influence it towards either good or ill, to reawaken religion or add culture, we must look to the child who is omnipotent."[101]

Montessori's lives have been laid before you, pointing to where her life choices intersected with feminist beliefs and leadership skills. A more detailed discussion of her leadership abilities relative to the implantation of her method in America will be discussed in Chapter Four.

We have seen many struggles in Montessori's lives. These were rarely economic. Her struggles were personal and cerebral. Her motivation was to define herself as an individual, an autonomous woman, irrespective of the conventions, norms, and expectations of her family or the larger society. Her conscious motivation was to utilize her leadership and method of education to create a more peaceable world.

Feminist biographer Liz Stanley thinks "that the way to do justice to women's lives is to see biography as a kaleidoscope: 'each time you look you see something rather different.'"[102] Initially, I saw Montessori as a rebel, who knew her goals and acted upon them in spite of family and societal objections. Quite frankly, this is one of the reasons that I was first attracted to her life. Then, I viewed her simply as a model of leadership and change. Today, I celebrate Maria Montessori's lives and the fact that she overcame the stifling conventions put on women of the late nineteenth century and succeeded in establishing her own voice for all to hear and follow. Almost one hundred years ago Charlotte Perkins Stetson said, "the world moves by means of some people's seeing farther than others and gradually inculcating their ideas in the minds of others."[103] Maria Montessori, the rebel, the feminist, the leader surely was one of these people.

NOTES

1. Maria Montessori, "Dr. Montessori Talks of her Mode of Auto Education," The *New York Times*, (December 7, 1913): X, 12,1.
2. Jane Kramer, "The Invisible Woman," *New Yorker*, (February 26, 1996): 136.
3. May Sarton, *Journal of Solitude*, (New York, 1977), 60.
4. Rita Kramer, *Maria Montessori: A Biography*, (New York: G. P. Putnam & Sons, 1976), 22.
5. J.P. Kirsch. "Sts. Thecla" *The Catholic Encyclopedia*, (New York: Robert Appleton Company, 1912): New Adventvent:http://www.newadvent.org/cathen/14564a.htm. Retrieved May 11, 2009.
6. Mary Garrard, http://www.efn.org/~acd/Artemisia.html., 1.
7. Valeria Babini and Luisa Lama, *Una Donna Nuova*, (Milano, Italy, 2000), 34.
8. Ibid., 35.
9. Ibid.
10. Maria Montessori, *San Francisco Call and Post*, August 9, 1915, n.p. This article was translated from the Italian by Ettore Patrizi, editor of *L'Italia.* Teachers College Special Collections, Series 10.5, Folder 9. This collection is now housed at the Thomas J. Dodd Research Center, University of Connecticut, Storrs, Connecticut.
11. Esther Pohl Lovejoy, *Women Doctors of the World*, (New York: The Macmillan Co., 1957), 203. Babini and Lama, "*Una Donna Nuova*, 38.
12. Tonzig, Maria, "*Quaderni Per La Storia Dell'Universita di Padova*," Padova, Italy: Antenore, (1973): 13.
13. Letter to author from Daniela Negrini, University of Bologna, July 3, 1996.
14. Letter to author from Gino Ferretti, University of Parma, June 8, 2009.
15. Babini and Lama, *Una Donna Nuova*, 38.
16. Maria Montessori, Speech at *SocietuAssociazione Femminile in, Der Internationale Kongres fur Frauenwerke und Frauenbestrebungen (Berlin: 19 bis 26, September 1896)*, 47. Translated by Dr. Armin Schadt, Professor Long Island University.
17. Kate Campbell Hurd-Mead, M.D., A *History of Women in Medicine*. (Haddam, CT: The Haddam Press, 1938); H.J. Mozans, *Woman in Science*, (Cambridge,

MA: The M.I.T. Press, 1913); Esther Pohl Lovejoy, Women Doctors of the World, (New York: The Macmillan Company, 1957).

18. Vittore Rava, *Le laureate in Italia*. Notizie statistiche, (Rome: Cecchini, 1902), 634–654.

19. Babini and Lama, *Una Donna* Nuova, 40.

20. Ibid., 37.

21. Ibid.,38.

22. Ibid., 108.

23. Kramer, *Maria Montessori: A Biography,* 92.

24. Babini and Lama, *Una Donna Nuova*, 108.

25. P. Boni Fellini, Cited in Babini, *Una Donna Nuova*, 108–109.

26. Carole Elizabeth Adams, *Women Clerks in Wilhemine Germany: Issues of Class and Gender,* (Cambridge: Cambridge University Press, 1988), 41–42.

27. Babini and Lama, *Una Donna Nuova*, 50.

28. Ibid., 47–48.

29. Maria Montessori, Speech at *Der Internationale Kongres* in Berlin, 1896, 48.

30. Ibid.

31. Ibid.

32. Maria Montessori, Speech at *Der Internationale Kongres* "Wages of Laboring Women," 202–203.

33. Ibid., 204.

34. Ibid.

35. Ibid.

36· Ibid., 208–209.

37. Ibid., 210–211.

38. Ibid. 211–212.

39. Kramer, *Maria Montessori: A Biography,* 56.

40. *Maria Montessori: A Centenary Anthology: 1870–1970.* (AMI/USA), 14.

41. Kramer, *Maria Montessori: A Biography,* 73–77.

42. Babini and Lama, *Una Donna Nuova*, 61.

43. Ibid., 60.

44. Ibid., 65.

45. Ibid., 78–80.

46. Ibid., 86.

47. Maria Montessori, "Child Psychology," *Times Educational Supplement*, October 9, 1919, 512.

48· Maria Montessori, *Discovery of the Child* (Adyar, Madras, India,1966).

49. Annarita Buttafuoco, "Motherhood as a political strategy: the role of the Italian Women's Movement in the creation of the *Cassa Nazionale di Maternita*," in Gisela Block and Pat Thane, eds. *Maternity and Gender Policies: Women and the Rise of the European Welfare States, 1880s-1950s.* (London: Routledge, 1991), 178–179.

50. Franca Pieroni Bortolotti, "A Survey of Recent Italian Research on the History of Feminism," *The Journal of Italian History,* (1, Winter 1978), 512–514.

51. Babini and Lama, *Un Donna Nuova*, 135.

52. Ibid., 235.

53. Horatio Pollock, "Notes on the Development of the Montessori System," *American Education*, (17, January 1914), 268.

54. Maria Montessori, *The Montessori Method*, (New York, 1964), 66.

55. Ibid.

56. Ibid., 63.

57. Ibid., 65.

58. Ibid., 69.

59. Pearl L. Boggs, "The Eternally Feminine in the Montessori System," *American Childhood*, (May, 1917): 195.

60. Ibid., 196.

61. Maria Montessori, *The Montessori Method*, 86.

62. Frederick C. Griffin, ed., *Woman as Revolutionary*, (New York: New American Library, 1973), XIII.

63. *The New York Times*, (December 7, 1913), 12.

64. *The New York Times*, (Section III, May 17, 1914), 2.

65. "Dr. Montessori in London," *Times Educational Supplement*, (September 4, 1919), 453.

66. Maria Montessori, *Education for a New World,* (Adyar, Madras, India, 1963), 28.

67. Slides from my collection, (1970), Nordweg, Holland; Translated in "Maria Montessori, A Life Devoted to Children," *Milwaukee Journal*, Teachers College Special Collections, Box 11, Series 10.1, Folder 1.

68. "The Montessori System," *Times Educational Supplement*, (January 6, 1919), 30.

69. "The Montessori Method in Italy," Times Educational Supplement, (December 23, 1922), 560.

70. "Children Under Six—Dr. Montessori's Views," *Times Educational Supplement*, (June 24, 1922), 295.

71. Tannenbaum, E.R., *The Fascist Experience: Italian Society and Culture, 1922–1945.* (New York: Basic Books, Inc., 1972), 154.

72. Ibid., 156.

73. *The Montessori Magazine*, (1, no.1, December, 1946), 13.

74. Halperin, S. William, *Mussolini and Italian Fascism*, (Princeton, NJ: D.Van Nostrand Company, Inc., 1964), 146.

75. Howard W. Schneider, *The Fascist Government of Italy*, (New York: D. Van Nostrand Company, Inc., 1936), 144.

76. Tannenbaum, *The Fascist Experience,* 151–152.

77. Dennis Mack Smith, *Italy*, (Ann Arbor: University of Michigan Press, 1959), 423.

78. "Mussolini and Montessori: An Established Principle," *Times Educational Supplement*, (April 4, 1925): 137.

79. Marjan Schwegman, *Maria Montessori*, (Bologna, Italy: Il Mulino, 1999), 103–104. In Italian and Dutch.

80. "*Il movimento Montessori a Napoli*," *Vita Dell'Infanzia* (xvi, no.3, *Marzo*, 1967), 13–14.

81. "*L'Idea Montessori,*" *Times Educational Supplement*, (June 11, 1927), 271.

82. Maria Montessori, "Nursery Schools and Cultural Environment," *Catholic School Journal 52*, (October 1952): 54A-55A. This is a series of excerpts culled from articles written for *UNESCO Features* in May 1952.

83. Max Gallo, *Mussolini's Italy: Twenty Years of the Fascist Era*, (New York: Macmillan Publishing Company, Inc., 1964), 220–221.

84. Richard Collier, *Duce: A Biography of Benito Mussolini*, (New York: The Viking Press, 1971), 104.

85. Tannenbaum, *The Fascist Experience,* 161.

86. Dennis Mack Smith, *Italy*, 180.

87. Max Gallo, *Mussolini's Italy*, 215.

88. Ibid.

89. Perry R. Wilson, *The Clockwork Factory: Women and Work in Fascist Italy*, (Oxford: Clarendon Press, 1993), 2.

90. Ibid., 4.

91. Renzo De Felice, *Mussolini il duce: Gli Anni del consenso, 1929–1936*, (Turin, Italy: Giulio Einaudi Editors, 1974), 110.

92. Schwegman, *Maria Montessori*, 108.

93. Roy MacGregor-Hastie, *The Day of the Lion: the Life and Death of Fascist Italy, 1922–1945,* (New York: Coward-McCann, Inc., 1963), 151.

94. Collier, *Duce: A Biography,* 102.

95. Ibid., 66.

96. Laura Fermi, *Mussolini*, (Chicago: The University of Chicago Press, 1961), 274–275.

97. Kramer, *Maria Montessori*, 327.

98. Maria Jervolino, "*Incontri con Maria Montessori,*" *Vita Dell'Infanzia*, (xi, no. 5–6, May–June, 1962), 6.

99. *Maria Montessori: A Centenary Anthology*, 19.

100. Ibid., 47.

101. Montessori, *Education for a New World,* 28.

102. Liz Stanley in Theresa Iles, *All Sides of the Subject: Women and Biography*, (New York: Teacher's College Press, 1992), 64.

103. Charlotte Perkins Stetson, "The Women's Congress of 1899," *The Arena*, (22, September, 1899), 348.

Chapter Three

The Peripatetic Life of Nancy McCormick Rambusch

As the founder of the American Montessori Society, Nancy McCormick Rambusch was one of the keynote speakers at the first AMS conference I attended in Philadelphia in 1968. Her rapid-fire speech, her extraordinary vocabulary, and her remarkable sense of humor overwhelmed and reenergized me at the same time. My doctoral dissertation would involve in large part Nancy's role in reintroducing Montessori education to America. I think I wrote down every word that came out of her mouth whether I understood it or not. Two years later, I actually met Nancy. Meeting her has been described as being like going to a good Broadway show where you are always on the edge of your seat trying to keep up with the dialogue. She was the woman who in the June 1963 issue of Newsweek had been referred to as "the red-haired dynamo." I had carefully planned the words I would use to tell Nancy about all I had studied about the diffusion of innovations.

At first sight she appeared shorter to me than she had at the podium two years before and her red hair also was much shorter than it had been. I felt a bit intimidated.

"Let's go talk at the Clam Box", she said, referring to a restaurant in Cos Cob, Connecticut to which I would return many, many times. They served a five-course meal after which I felt Thanksgiving-stuffed. "Dessert?" the server inquired. "No, I'm too full," I replied. "It comes with the meal," she responded. Why of course I would eat that great big cream puff covered in chocolate sauce. Why not? Food for thought—both literally and figuratively? This was the first of many times I would break bread with Nancy and each time I would come away filled with food and ideas. If Nancy weren't dieting and espousing the benefits of brown rice, she was eating and advocating provocative ideas that crammed my head with exciting thoughts of educational innovation and change.

Over this first lunch I began to talk to Nancy about the role leadership played in innovation; specifically, I spoke to her about her leadership role in the Montessori movement. Her big brown eyes got even larger. She became quite excited. Although Nancy spoke more rapidly than most people had the capacity to listen, she also was an intent listener who was able to process more quickly than most people were able to talk. She seemed to quickly anticipate the formal academic language I so wanted to share with her in order to demonstrate my knowledge about innovation diffusion. In a few short minutes, Nancy brought to life the past twelve years in which she had reintroduced Maria Montessori to the American public. I began to feel left behind. However, all the dry, technical terms I had so fervently studied now became drenched with real meaning. I had read that leaders who make extensive use of all types of media should be considered of higher quality than those who make lesser use of it. Here sat the "media guru" munching on enormous cream puffs and putting into precise language how she had used the media unknowingly, intuiting how innovation and diffusion transpires. After eating all that food, I remember practically having to be rolled away from our first meeting, all the while feeling affirmation from Nancy that I was on the right track. Recently, in reading remembrances of Nancy, I found many people felt the way I had that first day. Others recalled, "She gave language to our thoughts and actions," or "She illuminated . . . thoughts and visions and gave them language."

Nancy's use of language was extraordinary, both verbally and in writing. Friends had told me about Nancy's great ability to synthesize ideas and make them uniquely her own. The morning after our first meeting, Nancy telephoned to tell me she had "written two chapters last night" about her role as a leader in the reestablishment of Montessori in America. I hoped the good food and discussion with me had inspired this writing. To me, good food and great thoughts will always recall fond memories of the inimitable Nancy McCormick Rambusch.

Nancy Ellen McCormick was born in Milwaukee, Wisconsin on April 29, 1927. Her mother, Kathleen Wright, unlike many women of her time, was a college graduate. She held a masters degree in English and became a high school English teacher. Thomas McCormick, her father was an ophthalmic surgeon and a classics' scholar. Together they provided a home atmosphere that was "about the mind." "Intellectual accomplishments were very much valued in the McCormick household."[1]

When Nancy was six-weeks-old her father discovered that she had been born with one leg shorter than the other as the result of a double circulatory system on one side of her body. She was shuttled from one specialist to another during which time she was encouraged to take the "bumps and bruises" of childhood.[2] She often overheard the pitying comments of sympathetic friends and relatives. She recalled that her father told her, "Nancy, everyone's crippled, but some show it on the outside."[3]

Although Nancy forewarned her audience that the nature of "retrospective reflection, frequently gives way to nostalgia, [and] nostalgia is a counterfeit emotion,"[4] her recollections provide an understanding of the development of the strong sense of competence and self worth Nancy developed during those early years in the McCormick household. She related, "I came from a family of five girls. I was the youngest. I was born crippled and when we recollected how we were as children we had very, very different experiences. I had more different experiences than my sisters and there were reasons for that. From the time I was very young my father would respond to suggestions I had about what I wanted to do with the statement, 'If Nancy thinks it's a good idea, it's a good idea'."[5]

It wasn't until Nancy was thirteen years old, that her father, while reading a medical journal, discovered the surgeon that he and his wife had diligently sought for all those years. Nancy was faced with a major decision regarding her physical condition. The surgery her father had uncovered was experimental and would use bone to create a pin to shorten one of her legs. Whether or not to attempt the surgery was given to Nancy to decide, further indicating the faith her parents held in her decision- making abilities. She went ahead with the surgery and spent one year in a body cast. The surgery was a success, and she mused, "I walked away from my hospital bed and out into life." She theorized that during her recuperation period she had skipped adolescence and had gone from being a child to being an adult. "Children who are born with handicaps and live with them are very tough people," she said.[6]

Nancy's father had a sensitive ear to grammar whether in English or Latin. Constant corrections at the dinner table led all of his daughters to become "paragons of correct grammar," but Nancy informed her mother if her father didn't refrain from all of these corrections she wouldn't let him help her with her Latin. She recalled, "If I got an absolute ablative wrong or I identified something incorrectly, he'd go into overdrive and really it didn't matter if it were a dative or an ablative, but I said to my mother if he cannot control himself he cannot help me."[7] Nancy was beginning to recognize there were choices she could make to control her own life.

She also learned there were some issues which were not up for discussion. Her early schooling had been at St. Robert's parochial school in the Milwaukee area. In response to her criticizing a nun's pronunciation of the mountains between France and Spain as "PY Ariens," her father said "that was sister's best information." Nancy recollected that was a good answer "for a nine year old with a smart mouth." Years later she noted she was "very dissatisfied with the narrow type of religious and intellectual formation received as a school child in a parochial setting."[8] Apparently, her teachers thought more of her than she did of them. About twenty-five years later, Nancy received a letter from her fourth grade teacher stating she had missed Nancy when she was in Los Angeles and inviting her for dinner if she were to come again.[9]

Both her all-girls' family and single sex-schooling, she admitted later in her life, positioned her "heavily into autonomy." Being born the last of five sisters gave her the "opportunity to appreciate women." She recalled she was "doubly fortunate in attending a single-sex secondary school, where as prefect of the sodality and the senior voted most likely to succeed, I was able to give full rein to my emergent gift of religious enthusiasm, intellect and leadership."[10]

Formal schooling was a way of life for Nancy, as it had been for her mother and father before her. She began her studies at Dominican University, formerly Rosary College, in River Forest Illinois. Her father influenced her to take Greek in addition to a full program. Nancy later transferred to the University of Toronto in Canada, where she majored in English language and literature, like her mother. She received her Bachelor of Arts degree with honors in 1949.

Recalling the rigorous curriculum at St. Michael's College at the University of Toronto, Nancy said she found herself "in a cerebral paradise of delicious, albeit temporary, androgyny." She came in contact with people attempting to make a case for male domination based on the subordination of women due to "women's defective nature." She added, "I paid little attention. Protestation of the superiority of men over women meant relatively little to me up to that point, I had seen scant empirical evidence to support such a claim."[11]

Nancy's upbringing had prepared her to ignore the mid-40's rhetoric of the returning World War II veterans and some of the faculty at the University of Toronto. Professor J. Dore, however, would have a lasting influence on her life and thus the lives of many other Americans, including me.

Nancy wrote that she "happened" upon the writings of Maria Montessori.[12] J. Dore, her psychology professor had sparked her interest when he drew parallels between Thomas Aquinas' dictum, "there is nothing in the intellect that is not first in the senses," and Montessori's similar beliefs. Nancy was facile in French as well as English because this "happening" was a new French translation of *The Montessori Method* by Mme. Jean Jacques Bernard, a Montessori disciple. Nancy remembered being "struck by the freshness of Montessori's ideas and their obvious absence from the American child-rearing scene, as [I] perceived it, from [my] twenty-year-old vantage point."[13] She recalled before reading this book, "I thought Montessori was either an aging Italian singer or an antipasto."[14] Nancy was one step ahead of me. At least she knew Montessori was someone or something Italian. I had thought she was Indian.

While at the University, Nancy met Robert Rambusch, which she called, "a singular blessing and certainly the most important event of all that happened in those years."[15] They shared an involvement with the Young Christian Students and the ideal of the intellectual life.

After her graduation from the University of Toronto, Nancy went to Paris on a scholarship (*Bourse d'Etudes du Gouverment Francais*), where she studied French Literature and Romance Philology at the University of Paris. While there, in an effort to improve her French skills, she went to the movies a great deal. This practice appears to have become a life-long pattern and she often went to the "flicks" (as she called them) in New York and elsewhere, sometimes going to different movie theaters on the same day."[16]

On a regular basis she also stopped by to chat with two of her French friends, a Place St. Sulpice bookseller and his wife. "Discussions ranged from Anaxagoras to Claudel, politics to poetry." She was fascinated by the Montessori schooling their children were receiving.[17] Although she admitted that during her two years in Paris she spent little of her time worrying about the education of young children, she did take advantage of the opportunity to observe the children's Montessori school for herself. The seeds of Montessori's ideas were germinating.

On June 2, 1951, Nancy Ellen McCormick married Robert Edward Rambusch. By this time Bob was an artist engaged in working with interior church designs.

On May 17, 1952, Nancy and Bob Rambusch became the parents of a son, Rob. On the day before she went into labor Nancy took her final exams for her master's degree in Early Childhood Education at Columbia University. She declared, "My life was totally transformed. It takes only one swallow to make a spring and the first child to make a mother."[18]

My health education teacher said, "What's good for the mother is good for the child," and Joanna in Holtby's novel *The Land of Green Ginger* phrased it this way, "I think I can do the best for the children by doing the best for myself. . . . The children depend on me to protect them and be wise for them."[19] Nancy, also, did not deceive herself into thinking it was necessary to stay home all the time to tend to her son and husband.

"When two people of independent minds marry, they must rely upon each other's tolerance, affection and support. Each must encourage, without jealousy, the full development of the other's gifts, each allow the other privacy, different interests, different friends. But they must share an intellectual and moral base."[20] This description of Virginia Woolf's marriage so fittingly describes the marriage of Nancy McCormick and Bob Rambusch.

Nancy's own views were explicit, courageous and prescient. She told a reporter, "We've educated women but haven't educated people to accept the consequences." When questioned about the role of a wife, she said there was confusion in American culture. Her definition was, "An equal partner in a society that is no longer patriarchal, or the Victorian ideal of the submissive wife," adding, [it] requires two people who believe this."[21] Bob Rambusch proved to be that equal partner she required.

In a speech entitled, "Woman and Catholic" delivered to a church group twenty-five years later, Nancy gave a retrospective on how she had felt and lived her life. "In addition to my categorical Catholic definition of married woman and mother, I am also a person who has, in the world's words, had a career. A more accurate description would be that I did not derive my social identity uniquely from my husband's accomplishments, as married women have done traditionally, but from my own."[22]

Many women today would view Nancy's actions as quite normal. In 1950's and 60's America they were considered iconoclastic. Perhaps her views on Catholic tradition would remain such today. She told the same audience, "My devotion to Mary has always been to her as the Blessed Mother, certainly not as wife. Mary represented for me that gift of total presence to her child that has been hailed as the aim of perfect motherhood." She decried the dictum of the church leadership in "its almost invincible inability to respond to new women's agendas in any other way than reframing issues in the form of female subsidiarity."[23]

Nancy went on to explain these views were held not only in the Catholic tradition but in the past one hundred years by the American middle class. During this period fathers were no longer at home but began working in the outside world. Therefore, "mothers", she said, "were to be the angels of the house, and educated women were enjoined to put their energies and gifts at the service of forming young minds and hearts."[24]

She brought to her marriage and to the birth of her children the perspective of having been raised in a devout Irish-American family with parents who "were both first generation Americans and incipient feminists." She recalled her mother had been an English Professor until her marriage. The birth of five daughters in seven years found her devoting all of her time to her children, adding her father would have found it "déclassé" for a young and ambitious physician to have his wife work. Nancy confessed that although her mother was a model of devotion to her husband and children, her restlessness as a woman "who considered herself unfulfilled, although married, infected all of her children."[25] Nancy recollected an earlier encounter at a summer camp in Illinois when she was fifteen years old. One of the leaders said "for Catholic women, there were only two choices, to think or to breed. That was what my mother had been told. I saw no reason, then or subsequently, that one could not do both. I knew of no ovarian impediment to speculative thought, nor have I since found one."[26]

Describing her motivation to go to Paris and further pursue the ideas of Maria Montessori, Nancy wrote, "As an intentional Catholic parent, I became committed to providing for my children the best possible education and, if I could, one very different from my own.[27] She elaborated on this idea years later. "Like many American Catholics, I saw no conflict in sustaining a fidelity to the church matched by trenchant criticism of its institutional arrangements." She continued, "My reverence for experience, borne of my child life as an outsider, inclined me toward philosophers celebrating personally-acquired rather than received wisdom."[28] One of these philosophers was Maria Montessori.

Nancy now turned her full attention to the education of her own children and in the process to the education of other children in America. Her total activism on behalf of her own children's education was to become the rebirth of Montessori education in the United States. Years later she would tell an audience, "If it appears excessive for me to have started a social movement merely to satisfy my need to give my own children the best possible education, I can only say, retrospectively, that it was completely consistent with the energetic and ambitious person that I was."[29] Eight years earlier, when questioned about the same subject matter, Nancy had declared, "Hell, I was the women's movement," adding that she believed it was important for children to witness a parent who is committed to a "super ordinate goal."[30]

In 1952, before her son Rob was a year old, and with her husband Bob's financial and moral support, Nancy returned to Paris to attend the Tenth Annual International Montessori Congress sponsored by the French government at the Musee Pedagogique. Nancy had hoped to meet Maria Montessori, who was scheduled to be at this conference, but Montessori had died in May of that year. Instead, she met Mario Montessori there. She believed he was the logical person to approach since he had been left the "family business," the Montessori movement. She added, "It seemed reasonable to me at the time I met him, that Mario Montessori should control the social movement of which his late mother had been the cause and the center."[31] Nancy told him she was interested in establishing a "Montessori type" school in the United States. He responded, "Madame, there is no 'Montessori type' school, there is only a 'Montessori school."[32] Mario encouraged Nancy's desire to bring Montessori education back to the United States. She admitted she was unsure of the past history of Montessori in America, so when she returned to the States she researched this area and published an article in the first issue of *Jubilee* Magazine, "Learning Made Easy." *Jubilee* was a liberal Catholic publication which targeted a young educated audience. This article was the first on Montessori to appear in several decades. It was also the first of many Montessori articles that Nancy would write in the coming years.

Talks with Mario Montessori also inspired her to return to formal schooling. He convinced her to take Montessori training classes in London. In the fall of 1954, pregnant and accompanied by her young son, Nancy returned to Europe to complete the "authorized" Montessori Elementary Course. Once again her husband stayed in New York to support their travels while backing her commitment to further her education.

She was the first American after World War II to be trained in London. She completed the Montessori Primary Course with "Distinction." If one takes Nancy's description of the course seriously this was probably not very difficult. Course content, according to her, was similar to that offered during Maria Montessori's lifetime, "bereft of her genial presence." The prime focus of the course was unstructured experiences with the "didactic apparatus," never demonstrated with children present. A secondary focus of the course "was on the transmission of Montessori folklore and myths in the form of anecdotes of Montessori's life and work, which were delivered with the reverence and solemnity usually accorded the scripture." Few members of the class were university graduates while some had not even completed high school. "There appeared to be no academic prerequisites for the Montessori training."[33]

The Rambuschs' daughter Alexandra was born on May 14, 1955. One wonders if there were some spiritual connection between Nancy's completion of programs and the birth of Rambusch children. Her husband planned to join her when the baby was born. But, the *Milwaukee Sentinel* reported, "His independent wife [wrote], "Let's use the money and go to Spain for semester break. I'll have the baby by myself."[34]

After the break, Nancy promptly enrolled in the Montessori Elementary course, the second level of training for teaching children between the ages of six and twelve. These were the two Montessori training courses recommended by Mario Montessori.

On her return to the United States in 1955, Nancy set up a "Montessori type" play group in her home in Greenwich Village for her own children and five or six others, contrary to the admonition of Mario Montessori. Montessori education, initially introduced to America by Maria Montessori, had flourished during the early part of the twentieth century but had virtually vanished from the United States from the mid 1920's until Nancy began this Montessori play group in her home. Montessori schools, however, did continue to thrive in many other countries around the world. This play group continued to meet for about two years.

During this time as the seeds continued to grow, Nancy remained in contact with Mario Montessori. He sent her many visitors who had been involved earlier with the Montessori movement in Asia and Europe. He introduced her to Montessorians from both Europe and the United States who had been involved previously with the Montessori movement in Europe and America. Through further research Nancy learned about Emma Plank, Lilli Peller and Lisl Braun, all of whom were now living in the United States and had been close to Montessori in the past. She contacted these women but none was interested in a parent-centered Montessori movement. Nancy remained focused on her goal of bringing Montessori education back to America.

In 1956, the Rambusch family moved to Greenwich, Connecticut. There, Nancy sought out like-minded parents who wanted to be deeply involved with their children's education. Two of these parents were friends of the Rambuschs, John and Janet Bermingham. Having learned about Montessori education from Nancy, they became interested in starting a Montessori school in Greenwich.

Nancy's efforts to recruit other parents were markedly proactive. She wrote a series of articles for *Jubilee* introducing Montessori to America, spoke at any meeting, large or small to which she was invited, and spoke on radio and television in order to bring the Montessori message to the American public. She professed, "I was the Methodist circuit rider on the frontier, gathering Montessori enthusiasts into 'classes' and returning periodically to keep them committed and connected."[35] Nancy once described herself as Shirley Temple's mother trying to promote Shirley Temple. *Greenwich Time* described one of her "whirlwind" tours of seven cities: Syracuse, Cleveland, Milwaukee, St. Paul, Iowa City, Springfield, Illinois and Detroit."[36]

In all these lectures and writings, Nancy employed a method she called "psychic franchise." She explained this term as a technique in which one sells an idea back to a group of people who are already committed to the idea.[37]

The idea referred to was the academic climate of the 1950's, the anxiety about the state of American education spurred by the recent launching of the Russian Sputnik on October 4, 1957. She dovetailed the anxiety of these parents with the benefits of the Montessori system, designating this as a "grassroots parents' movement."[38]

Nancy has been given sole credit for reviving the Montessori movement in the United States by people with many divergent views. *Newsweek* referred to her as the "red haired dynamo of the Montessori revival."[39] The *Catholic Reporter* called her "the lady who started it all." [40] *Today*, a national Catholic magazine, reported an encounter with Nancy was "not a calming experience" as she was "single-mindedly" focused on the revival of the Montessori approach.[41] *The Washington Post* designated her as "the educator who is responsible for renewing this nation's interest in the Montessori Method of education."[42] Nancy, however, always attributed the reintroduction of Montessori education to "a small but pithy band of sassy, critical and articulate middle-class parents."[43]

Additionally, Nancy "located a small group of affluent Catholics who were dissatisfied with the local parochial schools and were interested in starting a Montessori school." These Catholic families she said "were persuaded that the parochial education awaiting their children was as monolithic in structure as it was in intent," adding these families "tended to have "sizeable, tightly-spaced families."[44] Her contention was that "Dissatisfaction with existing educational arrangements and affluence were to prove the prime ingredients in launching the new American Montessori movement."[45]

Nancy asserted Montessori education could have only been revived by an American. She believed she had an intuitive understanding of the culture and did not look at Montessori as a single solution. Many years later Nancy would relate to an audience, "much of what I did was quintessentially American. Like Margaret Fuller, who claimed an original relationship to the universe, I claimed such a relationship to the American culture."[46]

Therefore, she sought out the parents who would be most accepting of Montessori's ideas. These parents, she said, were agreeable to sending their children to a Montessori school that was a "blend of Christian humanism and nineteenth century scientific optimism."[47]

The connections Nancy made with these affluent Catholic families, many of whom had read her article on Montessori in *Jubilee* Magazine, combined with their own agendas for bettering their children's education, led to the founding of the first Montessori school in the second half of the century. One of these families was the Skakels who had established the Great Lakes Coal and Coke Company in 1919, from which they amassed their wealth. After the death of George Skakel and his wife Ann, their children wanted to do something as a memorial to their parents. They proposed turning their stable into a Montessori school.[48] The prime mover was their daughter Georgeann Skakel, the sister of Ethel Skakel Kennedy. Georgeann had become familiar with Montessori education through another sister in Ireland whose children attended a Montessori school there.

On September 29, 1958, Whitby school was founded in the Skakel's Greenwich, Connecticut stable-carriage house as the first Montessori school [since the revival] in the United States. *Time* reported, "It was founded by firmly anti-permissive Roman Catholics, and its old Montessori methods turn out to be a showcase of nearly every 'new' idea that U.S. education has lately discovered."[49]

Nancy's doctoral dissertation illuminated the significance of the Whitby name to the school's founders. She related a story told by Venerable Bede, an English Monk and scholar. As it is chronicled, the Abbess Hilda of the Whitby Abbey monastery in Yorkshire, England heard of a stable boy named Caedmon who had a mellifluous voice. Hilda invited him into the monastery so everyone inside could enjoy his great gift of song. Nancy wrote that this story was taken as "a paradigm of what American Catholic education had become. With all of its resources, it was leaving children 'outside' its enclosure, unmindful of their gifts."[50]

The presentation of Whitby school was not as a Catholic institution. Officially, however, it was under the jurisdiction of the Most Reverend Lawrence J. Sheehan of Bridgeport, Connecticut.[51] Nancy was appointed Headmistress of the school. The demands of this position included arranging lecture schedules and visitor observation days, meetings with parents, advising the burgeoning number of Montessori enthusiasts, listening to training course complaints and of course the mundane decisions as to where to put the flagpole and carpool concerns. Personal interests included "dishing out the perennial dime for daughter Alexandra's chance on a classmate's cat (That's all we need, Alexandra—a cat)."[52]

Her role as a parent was very important to Nancy. In a speech to a Catholic group that included high-ranking clergy, and in a rare moment of extreme humility, Nancy admitted, "I am an amateur as a parent. I don't know what the Mendelian proportion for being a professional parent is, but I know that I am falling far short of it."[53]

Later in the same speech, however, Nancy was more confident of the decisions she had made in her marriage and with her children to pursue professional goals alongside her maternal responsibilities. She conceded that many times parents view themselves in a stereotypical way. But, she said, "If we as parents trust ourselves, if we accept ourselves recognizing the tremendous burden of responsibility placed on us and the graces which marriage gives us to effect for ourselves and our children the development of all concerned in this dynamic relationship, perhaps we can embrace the reality of parenthood more positively than many of us feel confident to do left to our own devices."[54]

Her conclusion reflected the difficult decision she as a working woman in the late 1950s had embraced. She confidently stated, "What better use can young educated women make than to put their learning at the service of the child, to become more adept, to become more aware of the needs of the young child in order that the child and the Church be better served by their heightened perceptions."[55]

Whitby School, with Nancy at its helm, began in Greenwich, Connecticut on Cliffdale Road as the American Montessori Center in September, 1958. It had seventeen students ages three through seven and a faculty of two including Nancy McCormick Rambusch who also was the Headmistress. In 1959 Whitby moved its six to nine year olds to rented classrooms at the Sacred Heart School in Byram, Connecticut by which time it had seventy-five pupils enrolled.[56]

Cocktail parties and other similar events were held at the homes of wealthy benefactors to raise money to bring Whitby School to fruition.[57] Nancy was very successful in raising $260,000 in ten days to build this new fully equipped Montessori school.[58]

Five years later with an enrollment of just under 200 students Mrs. Royall O'Brien, Mrs. John McCooey and Mrs. Theodore Donahue would use this same money-raising technique to "help defray the operating deficit of the Whitby School," at its third annual Whitby Ball.[59] It is interesting to note that fifty years ago when this newspaper article was published, all of these women were referred to by their husbands' first names.

In 1960 Whitby took over its present thirty-eight acre location.[60] In that same year Nancy founded the American Montessori Society.

Prior to that, in 1959, Nancy began teacher training classes. She contacted Mario Montessori who sent her Elizabeth Stephenson, whom he deemed a "reliable" trainer. Nancy described the training as, "anecdotes about Montessori's life, repetitious statements from Montessori's written works and a standard set of procedures for the manipulation of the Montessori didactic apparatus." She concluded, "It was completely a-contextual, based on the assumption that children the world over were more alike than different."[61]

Although Nancy did not question the authenticity of the trainers, she believed there was a need for cultural accommodation. She wanted to place Montessori education into an American perspective. At this juncture, Nancy sought the expertise of City University/Queens College professor, John McDermott to accomplish this task. He argued that the premise of universality of children "for purposes of education displays a basic naiveté about the extraordinarily powerful and irreducible interrelationships between a culture and the child's development of a modality of consciousness."[62] He maintained that all philosophies had to be updated and made relevant for their time.

McDermott's concerns went still further. His assessment of the parents who were supporting Whitby School was that they demonstrated "far too parochial a perspective. They showed concern neither for the world's children nor the nation's children, just their own children."[63] He advised the newly formed American Montessori Society that the Montessori movement was just one of thousands of social movements in the United States. In helping to put

Montessori education into an American context, McDermott counseled the necessity for moving the Montessori system out of the private sector into the mainstream in order to have a successful educational and social movement. He envisioned a movement which reached all children from all cultures, not on the periphery of society but rooted in the public school system.

This view of the future needed to be put on hold as Nancy was now dealing with the immediacy of the proliferation of Montessori schools (Her leadership skills in this regard will be discussed in chapter five).

In June 1960 an ebullient young man, John P. Blessington (Jack) joined the staff of Whitby School. He recalled, "string marked the site of our first building when I arrived," ... [it was] an educational community which grew into a family center as Whitby focused on the growth and development of children and their parents."[64]

One month later, with the ground for Whitby already broken, Paul Czaja reminisced "Nancy signed me up right out of graduate school to work with the older children in Latin, creative writing, and in probably the first philosophy course for children in America."[65] Nancy's good judgment in hiring these two individuals would later serve her and the American Montessori Society well.

By the end of February 1960, the American Montessori Society, with its headquarters at Whitby School and Nancy McCormick Rambusch as its President, requested admission as a national society to the Association Montessori Internationale (AMI). This request was ultimately granted. The institutionalization of the Montessori movement in America and the controversy that surrounded it followed. Over the years heated debate and controversy ensued while Nancy continued to lecture and promulgate Montessori's ideas (See Chapter five). Nancy recognized from the beginning there would be major differences in a Montessori approach as opposed to the Montessori Method. She recalled the organization was named the American Montessori Society and not the Montessori American Society.[66]

She described the situation from her perspective and the hindsight of fifteen years:

> What actually existed at the heart of the 'international' Montessori movement was a scantily clad self styled emperor. Mario Montessori, as his mother's heir, attempted to control teacher training much as she had done in her life. The format for the training, however, was now reduced to anecdotes and demonstrations of the didactic apparatus, in the hands of disciples deemed sufficiently loyal to take such word, without distortion or modification, from the Mother Church of the aborigines."[67]

In the spring of 1962, Nancy published a book *Learning How to Learn: An American Approach to Montessori*. She described the reaction to this first book to placing Montessori education into a contemporary American setting, "Letters and people poured into Whitby from across the United States, demanding insistently that writers and visitors be given help in starting Montessori schools and teacher training programs."[68]

Nancy resigned as Headmistress of Whitby School in 1962, in order to devote more time to the day-to-day functioning of the American Montessori Society. The aforementioned Jack Blessington became Headmaster, where he remained until 1973 when Paul Czaja assumed the position. By 1966 with an enrollment of two hundred students, Whitby announced its plans to build the first Montessori high school in America by the following winter with the goal of doubling its enrollment.

On December 19, 1962 in a letter to Mario Montessori, Nancy resigned as President of the American Montessori Society effective July 1963. Hurt and disappointment are evident in her words, "This year for the first time, I received remuneration from the Montessori Society. In years past, I received none. I would prefer a relationship in which I could help in whatever way possible without continuing to assume the problems and absorb all the abuse that has been showered on me from every quarter."

She continued the letter with an explanation which displayed her honesty and integrity to Montessori and the Montessori Movement. She spelled out her beliefs, "It would have been easy for me, ten years ago, to have returned from Europe and submerged the name of Montessori and promoted these ideas in some other way. It was not my intent to do so. I think this would be criminal neglect of the genius of Dr. Montessori, as well as an intellectually dishonest move." Furthermore the letter revealed she was disheartened by the fact that she gave not only her time, "but that of my husband and children, over almost a decade."[69]

Royall O'Brien, at the tenth anniversary of the American Montessori Society, echoed the same themes, "Often misunderstood, even by those who followed her, often told 'it couldn't be done,' often abandoned . . . Nancy never gave up, never compromised, never retreated."[70]

Although very involved with the teacher training program and the promotion of Montessori education, Nancy knew it would be wise to have a degree in early childhood education so she entered Teachers College Columbia University. In 1963 she received a Master of Arts degree in Early Childhood Education. She began a PhD program, but did not finish it there.

In 1977, she received her Ed.D. from the University of Massachusetts at Amherst. Her doctoral dissertation was entitled, *Intuitive and Intentional Change Agentry*. It is an autobiographical detailing of her exploration into the literature on change and a description of her intuitive understandings during the reintroduction of Montessori to the United States. It also includes her acquired knowledge resulting in her intentional efforts to actuate change in three other situations.

While pursuing her doctorate, in the academic year 1973–1974, Nancy attempted to introduce a project called ANISA into the Hampden, Maine school system. Her reason for involvement in this venture was both because of its intellectual clarity and because of the opportunity it offered to work with Daniel Jordan, its creator, whom she portrayed as, "A rare person and a genuine innovator," adding, "Jordan can be compared to Gandhi in his effect on those working close to him, as I perceived the relationship."[71]

The ANISA model, which was designed for a secular school setting, "embraces all of the value systems through which man defines his relationships to three different types of environments, the physical, the social and the super-natural." Nancy wrote, "It might also be considered, in its educational guise, as a social movement." The model, through a three-year grant, was to be implemented at four sites, concurrently. The mission of the site teams was as conveyors of the content of the system as opposed to process. Now familiar with strategies of change agents, Nancy recognized "control and authority systems in bureaucracies do not work" therefore she utilized alternative strategies. During her first year, Nancy perceived that "top down' implementation would not succeed. She believed everyone needed to be involved in the decision-making and foresaw that the project was doomed to failure.[72]

Nancy and her team were confronted with introducing a model to teachers who had not chosen this system. The team worked, with her guidance, to lay the groundwork for change before thrusting new content on the teachers. Nancy's misgivings played themselves out. The entire team left after the first year. Nancy assessed the success, or rather failure, of that year, "What the ANISA team did was to help in the alteration of the social ecology of the school so that the model could 'take hold.'"[73] Its overall implementation, however, did not succeed.

Nancy's next venture into innovation took place in September 1974. Xavier University in Cincinnati had received a grant to establish a Montessori training program for elementary teachers and Nancy had been put in charge of it. In 1971 St. Mary's School in Hamilton, Ohio had begun a Montessori preschool program and hoped to expand to a Montessori primary unit. Nancy viewed this as an opportunity to test incremental change in a controlled environment.

She found a warm, friendly atmosphere run by knowledgeable adults and decided this would be a good school where she could work. The advantages of working there for her were the objectivity she could bring to the situation coupled with her nationwide experiences working with other social systems that had sought change. She served as a visiting Associate Professor in Xavier's education Department which gave her the power base and the freedom of movement necessary to be able to work at St. Mary's.

Explaining her compatibility there she wrote, "The whole American Montessori movement had been built on a Catholic 'educated parent' constituency. I was very much at home at St. Mary's because of my background and St. Mary's was very much at home with me."[74]

Once again she applied her knowledge of what had now become intentional Change Agentry. She incorporated modeling, acquired relevant resources, and practiced observation, dialogue and feedback convincing the teachers of the benefits of the ultimate proposed goal; *i.e.,* Montessori-izing" the program. After one year, the length of her contract, she assisted the staff in the process of '"stabilizing the innovation and generating self-renewal."[75]

Both St. Mary's and Nancy benefited greatly from their association. In the years after her work there, St. Mary's converted completely to a Montessori program for primary through the intermediate grades, and its enrollment increased to the point where they were no longer able to accept more children into the program. Nancy prided herself on her work. She wrote, "I got what I wanted as a change agent, the chance to demonstrate to colleagues at Xavier and in the Cincinnati Public Schools that change can occur most effectively when it is planned in manageable, incremental steps."[76]

In 1975, when the Cincinnati school system sought alternative means of desegregating its schools voluntarily, Nancy believed Montessori alternative schools might be the answer. Montessori preschool education had previously taken a strong hold in the Cincinnati area. Guided by the thought that Montessori education is 'elitist' in the minds of many, Nancy believed that "bringing Montessori education into the public schools signal[ed] the introduction of private school quality education into the public sector."[77] The environment was ripe for such an alternative.

More than a decade before, McDermott had predicted, "If Montessori's insights can be adapted to the demands of public education, then the revival so patiently nurtured by Nancy Rambusch and others will make a permanent contribution to American education." If not, he said, "This movement may soon have the dubious distinction of having suffocated itself twice in a half-century."[78] Insisting that Montessori could not survive as a predominantly Catholic experience, they urged that the movement seek a broader economic, religious and pedagogical base or it would always remain a cult on the fringes of American education. Nancy realized her dream and that of John McDermott in 1975 with the development of the first public Montessori school in America in Cincinnati, Ohio.

The easy part of the task was convincing parents to enroll their children in a Montessori public school. A waiting list developed quickly. The more difficult challenge came when attempting to plan the program with the superintendent and teachers when no building principal had been selected yet. In Havelock's terms, during this stressful period Nancy served as catalyst, solution-giver, resource-linker, and process-helper simultaneously.[79] When a principal whose philosophy was in keeping with Montessori principles was finally chosen, the teachers, who were Montessori-trained preschool teachers and had no real experience with American Montessori elementary curriculum, wanted to know who was in charge. The principal was there to manage the school. Rambusch was there to ensure the school was an American Montessori alternative. They needed to work together. She noted, "The 'installation' year at Children's House (the name chosen for the alternative school) reflected problems endemic to any beginning innovative effort, problems of exhaustion, extrapolation and acculturation."[80] The team experienced curriculum problems and major encroachment of traditional public school practice upon innovation.

The first year was very hard for all involved. The teachers having been trained at Xavier University for the Montessori elementary curriculum, prepared all summer for the students' arrival. They were physically and mentally exhausted before the term even began. Their inexperience combined with the inexperience of the students in a Montessori program led to "mercurial mood swings" and the staff settling for less than they had originally hoped for. Nancy summed it up, "Because the Children's House staff hoped for so much, it saw its limited first-year attainments as a deficiency, rather than an inevitability. The tendency of the disciple is to feel inadequate to the message of which he is the unworthy bearer."[81] Test scores for the five-year-olds were good but the other children did not succeed as well. Teachers believed there was too much attention being paid to test scores during the first year of the program. Despite the problems that surfaced during the initial year and in spite of Nancy's recommendation, Children's House expanded to a second site the following year.

Evaluating the nature of this effort, Nancy wrote, "Until we started Children's House, there was no such thing as an American Montessori public school. We had no mental picture of what such a school *had* to be like. Rather we had a clear picture of what we did not want it to be." Some Board members were willing to accept any innovation as long as it met the standards for the upcoming desegregation suit. Nancy believed they "were creating a public school which violated both the canons of the system and those of traditional Montessori thinking." This school was a Montessori public school not a public Montessori school.[82]

It was time for Nancy to move on. Alexandra Rambusch has said, "My mother was always on her next great work."[83] Looking at the Curriculum

Vitae of Nancy McCormick Rambusch one wonders how she continued to maintain the high energy level she brought to each "great work." Alexandra explained her mother's remarkable ability to communicate and to teach. She told me her mom was "as interested in other people's ideas as she was in her own. She was able draw out and take seriously students' ideas and develop them in front of them." Ideas were exciting to her and she was able to recognize and affirm others for their ideas. Since her own intellectual focus was always on ideas she was generous in sharing her ideas and energies with others.[84]

From 1958–1963, Nancy assisted in the establishment of over four hundred Montessori schools in the United States and continued working with the teacher training programs for the American Montessori Society. During the years 1963–1965 she served as the Director of the Early Learning Project at the New York Foundling Hospital for institutionalized children. For the next two years she was the Supervisor of early childhood programs for the Mount Vernon, New York public schools and then went on to become Director of the Central Harlem Association of Montessori Parents.

In her next venture she worked as the Director of Development for Creative Playthings for two years while continuing with the Montessori teacher training program and serving as a Consultant to the U.S. Office of Education.

In 1970, anticipating the growing need for child care and cognizant of developmentally appropriate practices for young children, Nancy founded and directed a school called Child Minders in White Plains, New York. Once again she appealed to educated parents. Her brochure advertised, "Outside-of-family experiences for young children should relate to the aspirations and time tables of their bright, concerned conscientious mothers." She promoted an environment that went "well beyond Montessori in the repertoire of experiences it makes available to young children."[85]

I visited Nancy at this school, which was attractive, well-equipped, and an exemplary early childhood setting. I found its child-centered environment pleasing to the eye and all of the other senses. Nancy showed me books of all sizes that had been covered in fur so children would use their sense of touch while enjoying the pleasures of reading.

In 1958, she wrote, "When the teacher speaks, it is to say something that the environment cannot say."[86] Nancy planned this environment when she developed Child Minders. Apparently this venture was not successful because there is no mention of it in her Curriculum Vitae.

For the next five years Nancy devoted her time to studying techniques of intentional change, applying these methods, and acquiring a doctorate in education in 1977. She returned to New York and to Montessori education and worked as the Head of the Caedmon School (a Montessori school) in

Manhattan, but was once more looking for "her next great work." It came through the professional influence of David Elkind, noted child development specialist. They had met in the early sixties and had developed a friendship over the years. Elkind explained, "We began to see each other at conferences and to share our interests, concerns, and activities. Or rather, to share mine. Nancy was always extremely modest and did not talk about all that she was doing. On the other hand, she always encouraged me to talk about my latest writing and research projects and always made me feel that I was doing prize-winning work."[87]

In 1978, when Elkind became Chair of the Department of Child Study at Tufts University in Massachusetts, there were problems with the children's school there. He encouraged her to apply for the position of director. She did, although there had been some slight opposition from faculty because of her association with Montessori education. She became director of the children's school and also an Adjunct Associate Professor in the Department of Child Study. Elkind described her accomplishments:

> Nancy quickly revamped the school. Physically it was a mess, with materials from the school's inception stashed in corners that no one had ever bothered to clear out. She soon had the school organized not only educationally but administratively. The deficit was significantly reduced by raised enrollments and tuition. The staff became much more professional in their outlook and in their practice. In a short time, that school was a model of educational excellence.[88]

A good friendship between the two ensued with weekly luncheon meetings that Elkind described "as the bright spot in my week." He found Nancy to be a very private person. They didn't discuss families or gossip about faculty. To Nancy "conversation" [was] a didactic dance."[89] They talked about "education, about politics, and about [their] understanding of the writings of Piaget and Montessori." When Elkind decided to step down as Chairperson of the Department four years later, Nancy decided it was time for her to leave.[90]

Her formal education did not cease. She secured a Mid-Career and Post Doctoral fellowship at Yale University's Bush Center for Child Development and Social Policy and pursued post-doctoral studies from 1984–1986 in Child Care Policy Studies.

Nancy's next position, from 1985–1987, was as Director of Early Childhood education for the Agency for Child Development in New York City. Her responsibility was to oversee the organization and implement Project Giant Step, a program for four-year-olds.

She pursued many, many interests of hers in the ensuing years. She held numerous positions of leadership and was employed in a great variety of positions many of which took her geographically far from home, but Nancy always returned to her family. Alexandra said, "She was a superb mom. Mother chose a field where she could take us with her—we were able to be part of her life."[91]

In 1987, when Nancy took a position as an Associate Professor of Education at the State University of New York at New Paltz, Alexandra moved there with her. They lived in Walkill, New York while Alexandra pursued studies towards a doctorate. Two years, and nineteen presentations later, Nancy received her tenure and in 1994 she was promoted to Full Professor. Nancy told me she was very happy tucked away in the Catskill Mountains.

Yet she still sought to expand her horizons and those of the Montessori movement. An opportunity to do this arose in early 1994. Beginning in 1989, and continuing for five years, Nancy served as Director of Staff Development at the Princeton Center for Teacher Education. In that capacity she presented seminars and workshops for teachers and administrators and in the adult education program offered to parents.[92]

During this period, The Princeton Center for Teacher Education entered into a partnership with the Main Education Board of Kiev, Ukraine, headed by Borys Zhebrovsky. After the fall of the Soviet Union in 1990, he looked at the existing educational system in his country and saw many inadequacies. He envisioned an educational system that would strengthen Ukrainian independence. In 1992, at a European educational fair he observed a Montessori classroom. He recognized this as the answer he had been seeking for Ukrainian children. He returned to Ukraine and sought out people of like mind. One of these people was Tatiana Mykhalchuk who came to the United States in 1993 and contacted Marsha Stencel, head of Princeton Montessori School and Ginny Cusack, then director of the Princeton Center for Teacher Education about a teacher education program in Ukraine. Cusack, facetiously wrote, "At that time, we didn't know anything about Ukraine—or even where it was on a map."

But, she continued, they were fortunate to have Nancy McCormick Rambusch on staff who said training teachers was not enough. [They] "needed a larger vision." She encouraged them "to adapt Montessori philosophy to the Ukrainian culture and start a Montessori movement analogous to the American Montessori movement."[93]

With great excitement, Nancy began this project with Princeton University to bring Montessori education to Ukraine. "She always dreamed of leading a Montessori movement in another country, as she had in America."[94]

In June 1994, the Ukrainian team came to Princeton to meet Nancy. Cusack described the electricity of this encounter. "The energy flowing between the two visionaries, Nancy and Borys, dominated our meetings: Borys had the Ukrainian vision, Nancy had the experience to make the vision a reality."[95]

The meetings were emotional. Nancy made the point that lasting change takes time and there needed to be a commitment of at least ten years. She developed a plan for Montessori education in Ukraine but a sudden illness prevented her from carrying it through. In an email to Cusack, Borys wrote, "I am sure that the most powerful stimulus for the Ukrainian Montessori Project was our personal meetings with Dr. Nancy McCormick Rambusch. They were historic."[96] The project continued and in 2008 there were Montessori schools in fifteen regions of Ukraine.[97]

In October 1994, the Maria Montessori Lifetime Achievement Award was bestowed on Nancy by the Montessori Accreditation Council for Teacher Education. By this time she was so ill that Ginny Cusack accepted it on her behalf and Nancy requested that it be given to the Princeton Montessori Society.

Shortly thereafter on October 27, 1994, Nancy passed away from pancreatic cancer. Nancy and Bob Rambusch had been married for forty-three years when she died. He was always supportive of her career and her ventures. He explained, "Nancy and I kept distinct our individual professional interests and colleagues. A person interested in my field of worship and the arts approached Nancy and assumed Nancy was an active participant in my discipline, she gushed, 'You must be *so* involved in liturgy and art.' Nancy calmly responded to the enthusiast 'I am on the conjugal fringes of the liturgical movement.' I kept distance from Nancy's academic circles."[98]

In a letter written to Nancy's friends after returning from her memorial service at SUNY New Paltz and having met her academic colleagues, Bob reiterated this story. He added he was touched by the number of people who felt that Nancy was their "best friend." The letter continued, "I believe it was Nancy's ability to bring out the excellence in each person she met and they in appreciating their own personal worth and discovery . . . achieved their 'best.' So, naturally, Nancy must have been *their* best friend."[99] This ability to make people feel they and their ideas were valuable was a personality trait Nancy embodied. I, also, came away from discussions with my feelings validated.

Nancy and Bob's marriage worked for them and for their children. She once said "the best education for a marriage is to come from a happy family."[100] Theirs was a marriage of equality and a wonderful friendship with rules known only to Nancy and her family.

She touched so many people beyond her immediate family. Like Maria Montessori she was a private person who did not talk much about her family or herself, but as Bob Rambusch said so many people perceived her as their best friend. One person even got an intimate peek into her home. She reported, "She and Bob lived in a brownstone in Greenwich Village that was filled with art. (As a matter of fact, there was more art in her bathroom than in my entire house!)"[101]

It is inevitable that when one challenges the present state of affairs, as Nancy did, she will not often be nominated for the Ms. Popularity title. She is bound to cross swords with one opponent or another. Over the years the occasional personal or professional gibe would surface. Nancy described herself, "as a ruffler of feathers, a raiser of hackles, and a burr under the saddle of AMI, the AMS Board and any other body she confronted."[102] She said that being loved was not a high priority of hers.

Gil Donahue, who worked closely with Nancy, bemoaned what he saw as the one flaw in Nancy's leadership. Describing Nancy he wrote that she "was truly a charismatic person—with all the vision, creativity, and personal magnetism implied by that term. But her strength was also her weakness. Nancy was like a beautiful butterfly flitting from flower to flower, pollinating each one with new life, but never staying long enough to nurture any of them."[103]

After her untimely death, tributes to her filled the pages of an entire issue of *Montessori Life* and page after page in *Public School Montessorian*, all viewing that aspect of her that most closely reflected their own view of life. I have chosen to include some of the eulogies and celebrations of Nancy's life in order to highlight the different roles she played and to get a deeper look into her many facets concentrating on her as a woman, change agent and leader.

Bretta Weiss, like me, saw her as short. She phrased it this way, "She may be the giant of the world, but she certainly is short. In twenty-four years of Nancy watching I came to see how tall she really stood, but I remained in awe of the size of her intellect and the depth of her passions."[104]

Others, who themselves have since become very successful women, saw beyond the physical aspects of the woman. Each was influenced by Nancy's entrance into the wider world beyond the family before it was a commonplace thing for women to do. She served as a model of the possibility of combining a successful family life with an accomplished career. She was a mentor and an enabler to many women, helping to stretch their vision in ways they could never before imagine. She inspired many women to explore professional options outside the home. Kit Frohne Johnson, currently a marriage and family therapist acknowledged: "Nancy provided me with a brand new expanded role model for being a professional woman. . . . Nancy was the first woman I knew who mastered the art of combining family and career.[105] Lanaro echoed Johnson's sentiments. She reflected, "That a life could be led with passion and conviction and purposefulness in the public domain while having a fulfilling family life was a revelation to me."[106]

Joy Turner was determined not to become a teacher, "despite [her] school superintendent father's advice to [her] during a career-decision crisis that 'it's a good job for a woman.'" She added, "This from a man I adored for his nurturing of my independence, initiative and intellect. But it was Nancy, I think, who freed me to be the teacher I already was . . ."[107]

Nancy was very proud of the designation "change agent." She wrote, "My work as an innovator may be characterized by the metaphor, 'change agent,' which in the literature of applied social science has come to mean a person brokering change within institutional settings."[108] She examined Sarason's analysis of the elements of the change effort, "seen primarily as a function of some combination of a single individual's temperament, intellect and motivation," combined with the understanding of the 'Zeitgeist,' "the general intellectual, moral and cultural state of an era."[109] In retrospect, Nancy realized she had "utilized a combination of both" aspects of the definition.[110] This designation "change agent" can be found throughout the professional and lay literature when referring to Nancy. More importantly, though, "she exhorted us to be true believers in our work—to be change agents ourselves."[111] She "challenged us to shift our paradigms."[112]

Jack Blessington described Nancy's leadership skills, "She had a calling, and it was to lead people. She led those who wanted to move on—into charted territory that was new to them or into totally uncharted waters. She always seemed fearless and confident, so others followed."[113]

People invariably were inspired by Nancy's abilities as a woman before her time, a leader, and change agent. In summing up her impact, John Chattin McNichols wrote, "She was never content to accept the status quo for herself or for the child. . . . She challenged all of us to re-examine what we were doing with and for children."[114] Thousands upon thousands of children have profited from the immeasurable time and energy Nancy committed to early childhood education in America.

In Nancy's inimitable style, she once said, the "ten commandments are not engraved on the left ventricle."[115] She overcame a multitude of "thou shall nots" to discover herself and leave her indelible imprint on the world of education.

NOTES

1. Alexandra Rambusch, Telephone interview with Nancy McCormick Rambusch's daughter, April 18, 1995.
2. Mary Beth Murphy, "Scratch Parent, Find Educator," *The Milwaukee Sentinel*, (May 24, 1978): 9.
3. Ibid.
4. Nancy McCormick Rambusch, Lecture Series, "Being With Children," (Princeton, N.J: Princeton Center for Teacher Education, Session II, October 21, 1993). Tapes given to me by Ginny Cusak.

5. Rambusch, Lecture Series, Session I, (October 14, 1993).
6. Ibid.
7. Rambusch, Session II.
8. Nancy McCormick Rambusch, *Intuitive and Intentional Change Agentry*, Unpublished Doctoral Dissertation, (Ann Arbor: University Microfilms, 1977), 82.
9. "Letter from Sister Macrina to Nancy McCormick Rambusch," (January 22, 1962), Teachers College Archives, Box 9, Series 7.2, Folder 6.
10. Nancy McCormick Rambusch, Speech to Church group, "Woman and Catholic in 1986," (May 7, 1986). Sent to me by Robert E. Rambusch.
11. Ibid.
12. Rambusch, *Intuitive and Intentional Change*, 82.
13. Ibid.
14. Mary Beth Murphy, "Scratch Parent, Find Educator," 9.
15. Rambusch, "Woman and Catholic."
16. Ronald R. Koegler, M.D., "Jumpin' With Nancy," *Montessori Life*, (7, no.1, Winter 1995): 17.
17. Jane Mary Farley, "Milwaukeean Leads Revolution in the Three R's," *The Milwaukee Journal* (October 8, 1964): 4.
18. Letter to author from Robert E. Rambusch, June 19, 2007.
19. Winifred Holtby, *The Land of Green Ginger*, (Chicago: Cassandra Editions, 1977), 301.
20. Nigel Nicolson, ed., *The Letters of Virginia Woolf, Volume II: 1912–1922,* (1976), xiii.
21. Mary Flynn, "Headmistress," *Today: National Catholic Magazine*, (November 1961): 5.
22. Rambusch, "Woman and Catholic."
23. Ibid.
24. Ibid.
25. Ibid.
26. Ibid.
27. Rambusch, *Intuitive and Intentional Change,* 82.
28. Rambusch, "Woman and Catholic."
29. Ibid.
30. Murphy, "Scratch Parent, Find Educator," 9.
31. Rambusch, *Intuitive and Intentional Change,* 83.
32. Nancy McCormick Rambusch, Interview with author, Greenwich, Connecticut, July 8, 1970.
33. Nancy McCormick Rambusch, "The American Montessori Experience," *The American Montessori Society Bulletin*, (15, no.2, 1977): 8–9.
34. Murphy, "Scratch Parent, Find Educator," 10.
35. Rambusch, *Intuitive and Intentional Change*, 88.
36. *Greenwich Time*, "Whitby School Headmistress Now on Tour of Seven Cities, (March 17, 1960), in *Whitby School: Thirty Years*, 1989, unpaged.
37. Appelbaum, *The Growth of the Montessori,* 129.
38. Ibid.

39. "An Intellectual Leap," *Newsweek*: (June 24, 1963).

40. *Catholic Reporter* "Montessori Insights and American Children Today," (Section II, May 31, 1963): 10.

41. Flynn, "Headmistress," 3.

42. *The Washington Post*, (November 5, 1962): B8.

43. Nancy McCormick Rambusch, (1995). Mary Reuter, Princeton Center for Teacher Education, collected different quotes by Nancy McCormick Rambusch and shared them with author.

44. Rambusch, *Intuitive and Intentional Change,* 89.

45. Ibid., 86–87.

46. Rambusch, "Woman and Catholic."

47. Rambusch, *Intuitive and Intentional Change*, 89.

48. Marcy Raphael, Telephone Interview with author, June 21, 2007.

49. *Time*, (May 12, 1961).

50. Rambusch, *Intuitive and Intentional Change,* 87.

51. Appelbaum, *The Growth of the Montessori, 135.*

52. Flynn, "Headmistress, 4.

53. Nancy McCormick Rambusch, "Untitled Speech," (1962) 1. Box 9, Series 7.3, Folder 7, Special Collections, Teachers College, Columbia University.

54. Ibid., 3.

55. Ibid., 12.

56. *The Whitby School Handbook*, (May 7, 1961), unpaged.

57. John and Janet Bermingham, Interview with author, (September 2007).

58. Appelbaum, *The Growth of the Montessori,* 135.

59. Newspaper clipping, *Whitby School: Thirty Years,* (1989), unpaged.

60. Whitby School, Greenwich, Ct., pamphlet, n.d., p.1. All of Nancy McCormick Rambusch's materials refer to Whitby as a 37 acre site.

61. Rambusch, *Intuitive and Intentional Change*, 99.

62. John J. McDermott, Quoted in Rambusch, *Intuitive and Intentional Change*, 100.

63. Rambusch, Ibid., 100.

64. John P. Blessington, *Whitby School: Thirty Years*, (1989), unpaged.

65. Paul Czaja, Ibid.

66. Nancy McCormick Rambusch, Interview with author, August 22, 1970.

67. Rambusch, *Intuitive and Intentional Change*, 91–92.

68. Ibid., 89.

69. Nancy McCormick Rambusch, Letter to Mario Montessori, (December 19, 1962), AMS files. Cleo Monson shared these files with me. This collection is now housed at the Thomas J. Dodd Research Center, University of Connecticut, Storrs, Connecticut.

70. Royall D. O'Brien, "A Tribute to Nancy Rambusch on the 10th Anniversary of the founding of the American Montessori Society," (1970).

71. Rambusch, *Intuitive and Intentional Change,* 118.

72. Ibid., 129.

73. Ibid., 138.

74. Ibid., 142–143.

75. R.G. Havelock, *The Change Agent's Guide to Innovation in Education*, (Englewood Cliffs, New Jersey: Educational Technology Publications, 1973), 133, in Rambusch, *Intuitive and Intentional Change*, 149.

76. Rambusch, Ibid., 150.

77. Ibid.,152.

78. John J. McDermott, "An Intellectual Leap," *Newsweek*, (June 24, 1963): Reprinted by the American Montessori Society.

79. Havelock, *The Change Agent's Guide*, in Rambusch, *Intuitive and Intentional Change,* 162.

80. Rambusch, *Intuitive and Intentional Change,* 167.

81. Ibid., 169.

82. Ibid, 174 and 158.

83. Alexandra Rambusch, Telephone interview with author, January 25, 1995.

84. Alexandra Rambusch, Telephone Interview with author, April 18, 1995.

85. Nancy McCormick Rambusch, *What Kind of Approach to Children Does Child Minders Have?,* n.d.

86. Nancy McCormick Rambusch, "Freedom, Order and the Child," *Jubilee*, (5, April, 1958): 37.

87. David Elkind, "A Good Friend," *Montessori Life*, (7, no.1, Winter 1995): 20.

88. Ibid.

89. Nancy McCormick Rambusch, Quoted by Karen Wintres, "Remembering Nancy," *Montessori Life*, (7, no.1, Winter 1995): 16.

90. David Elkind, "A Good Friend," 20.

91. Alexandra Rambusch, Telephone interview with author, April 18, 1995.

92. Marsha Stencel, Letter on the death of Nancy McCormick Rambusch, (October 27, 1994), Special Collections, Teachers College, Columbia University.

93. Ginny Cusak, "Building Ukrainian Montessori from the Ground Up," *Montessori Life,* (20, no.2, 2008): 24.

94. Ibid.

95. Ibid., 25.

96. Ibid.

97. Ibid., 22.

98. Robert E. Rambusch, Letter, "Dear Friends of Nancy McCormick Rambusch", January, 1995. Sent to author by Robert Rambusch.

99. Ibid., 2.

100. Rambusch, "Untitled Speech," 2.

101. Kit Frohne Johnson, "Force of Nature," *Montessori Life*, (7, no.1, winter 1995): 18.

102. Nancy McCormick Rambusch, Quoted by Desmond Perry, "A Catalyst," Ibid., 16.

103. Gilbert Donahue, Correspondence with author, April 24, 1996.

104. Bretta Weiss, *Public School Montessorian*, 7, no.2, (1995): 10.

105. Johnson, "Force of Nature," 18.

106. Pamela Zell Lanaro, *Public School Montessorian*, (7, no.2):12.

107. Joy Turner, *Montessori Life*, (7, no.1, winter 1995): 6.

108. Rambusch, *Intuitive and Intentional Change*, 1–2.

109. Ibid., 8–9.

110. Ibid., 9.

111. Bretta Weiss, "A Change Agent," *Montessori Life*, (7, no.1, winter 1995): 11. Ginny Cusack makes a similar claim in the same issue, 28.

112. Dorothy Ohlhaver, Ibid., 18.

113. Jack Blessington, Ibid., 14.

114. John Chattin-McNichols, "A World Made Better," Ibid., 9. Bob Pickering, in "A Mover," Ibid., uses the same words, 16.

115. Rambusch, Princeton Lectures, Session II.

Chapter Four

Montessori and Her Method Come to America

"Be careful there's a tiger," I shouted as we made our way through the thick underbrush. "Wait, there's a panther, my four-and-five-year old friends yelled. We paused to allow the striped orange tabby and a black cat with white mittened paws and underbelly to pass by. Hour after hour we explored our imaginary jungle in the vacant lot across from our apartment houses in one of the outer boroughs of New York City. By late morning we were hungry so we left our jungle and went to eat lunch.

After lunch my friends and I played with our paper dolls. We punched out the cardboard dolls, cut out their clothes very carefully and then used the small tabs to place the paper outfits on the dolls. We spent time having them talk to each other, and we chatted among ourselves, envisioning the lives these paper dolls might have down the street playing with the neighborhood goats.

Then it was time for us to go to the playground down the block. There we swung on the swings, played on the see-saw and slid down the slides. Later we climbed the monkey bars daring each other to climb higher and higher. A game of tag or statues rounded out the day. We spun around making all kinds of poses until someone yelled "freeze," and then we stopped in the frozen position of a dancer, an animal or some equally imaginary figure.

It was almost time for dinner so we went back home and wound down with a game of jacks. "Onesies" was easy. "Twosies" was much harder for us, but we practiced and practiced until we became skilled at the game.

Before I went to sleep I read a book for awhile, and then my mom or dad sat at the edge of my bed and read me a bedtime story.

The next day I began the routine once more. Neither I nor any of my friends went to nursery school. There were no nursery schools in our neighborhood. Our mothers were home cooking hot meals and preparing afternoon snacks for us. We were our own nursery school. We knew what children should be doing. Self-regulation taught us that early in the morning we should play hard. We ran through our make-believe woods, developing our large motor and language skills. Then we used a quiet activity to increase our fine motor development while once again extending our imaginations and vocabulary. After that it was time for active play once more in order to build our large motor abilities. Jacks were a perfect quiet pastime to further extend our small motor skills and wind down from a very busy day. No day would be complete without the one-to-one adult/child relationship and the chance to fantasize still further through the use of literature.

We were not totally prepared for kindergarten when the time came for us to leave our make-believe worlds and begin a new life in school. There, we would learn new routines and learn to sit more than run, to be part of the group rather than independent thinkers, to eat when it was time to eat rather than when our bodies told us we were hungry and do lots more listening than talking. Why weren't Montessori schools available to us then? It would be many years before I would learn the history of the Montessori schools in America.

The history of education is basically a social history. Some have described it as a depiction of events involving the ideas of leading figures in the context of their times. My definition moves beyond just the ideas of leading figures and examines the paths leaders took in shaping history by their actions and interactions with the situations and people with whom they came in contact. This chapter will consider the educational setting and leading educational players in early childhood education the Montessori movement encountered during its inception and subsequent demise in American education.

Until after the turn of the twentieth century preschool education was essentially the concern of the family. Separate facilities for nursery schools were not established until about 1900. Although some nursery schools were set up in America by 1900, they did not become popular until after the First World War. Previously, parents had felt that these institutions were encroaching on the function of the home and family.

Many believe the growth of nursery schools was connected to the Child Study Movement which experienced its thrust during the last two decades of the nineteenth century. G. Stanley Hall published, in 1883, *The Contents of Children's Minds on Entering School.* Although not the originator of the movement, he coined the word "paidocentric" and from then on the child study movement was directed to a "child-centered" philosophy. This educational theory was scientifically oriented. Hall spoke of stages in the development of childhood .It was his theory that "ontogeny recapitulates phylogeny," *i.e.,* each human being must pass through all the stages of human evolutionary growth. In addition to advocating a more scientific attitude and interest in the child, those in the child study movement criticized the rigidity of the existent school system with its rote-learning and narrow curriculum, its method of grading, and its poor materials and furniture. It complained that the children were adjusted to the schools and not the reverse. It sought to learn about the different stages of children's development, their language and their moral and religious feelings at various ages.

The growth in technical knowledge of the pre-school child had increased so rapidly since the First World War that few parents could keep abreast of it unaided. Brubacher pointed out "The declared purpose of the movement (nursery school), however, was not to supplant the home but to supplement it."[1] Certainly, some complement was necessary.

In 1916, a cooperative nursery school was formed at the University of Chicago by a group of alumnae and wives of the faculty. Forest said, "They felt the need, which they could not fill in their own homes, of the beginnings of social contact, of group play, the chance at give and take, and the supervision at times of adults not the children's own mothers."[2]

By the 1920s, research center nursery schools were established, many in connection with universities and teacher training schools. Basically, the nursery school movement was a private one until the Depression in the 1930's, when the Federal government supported nursery schools in order to alleviate unemployment among teachers.

In 1939, approximately twenty years after its precarious beginning, there were 652,000 nursery schools in the United States. By 1959, this number had increased to 2,160,000.[3] The National Household Education Survey (NHES) depicts a steady increase in early education in America. By 1999, (the latest statistics available) they show 46% of all three-year-olds and 69% of all four-year-olds attending preschool programs.[4]

The kindergarten, too, was brought to the United States as a private institution. It was introduced by German immigrants prior to the Civil War. The teachings of Freidrich Froebel and his materials known as "gifts" were presented as a package. There are varied accounts of the first public kindergarten in America. Most sources, however, attribute the first public kindergarten to Susan Blow and William T. Harris in St. Louis in 1873.

Associations were formed to introduce the kindergarten to the American public. In 1876 at the Centennial Exposition in Philadelphia, kindergarten materials were displayed. This helped to further the movement. Kindergartens were also opened in settlement houses and welfare centers.

By 1880, the United States Bureau of Education reported more than two hundred public kindergartens in fourteen states. Five years later the number had doubled and they could be found in thirty-five states. Because of the financial depression of 1893 many had to be closed.[5]

After the establishment of Susan Blow's kindergarten in 1873, "except for transient lapses, as when patriots disowned it as a German menace during the First World War or as a waste of public money during the Great Depression, the kindergarten captured the American heart."[6]

Vanderwalker divided the growth of the kindergarten movement into two periods—"The Period of Introduction," 1855–1880 and "The Period of Extension," 1880–1917 (the year of publication of her book). These two periods she further subdivided into two periods. From 1855 until approximately 1870 she termed "the period of the German Kindergarten." In the next ten years she said the kindergarten was accepted by Americans as an institution and adapted by them to American conditions and American needs.

During the first phase of the "Period of Extension" (1880–1890), the kindergarten was accepted without question. From 1890 on, it began to be viewed more critically. Many teachers, she claimed, were demanding a "reconstruction of its theory and practice."[7]

Many breakaway groups were formed to reflect their own beliefs about what kindergarten was or should be. The controversy centered on the strict interpretation of Froebel by Susan Blow and her followers and the desire for change by Alice Temple and Patty Smith Hill and those who believed as they did. Hill lectured at Teachers College, Columbia University in 1904. In 1910, she became the head of the kindergarten department there. Under her direction, Teachers College became the recognized center and leader of the newer kindergarten movement.

This description of the two factions that existed in the kindergarten movement is a gross oversimplification of a great many factors that led to these very different views.

Vandewalker contended the entire school pattern in the United States was influenced by the introduction of the kindergarten. It prepared the way for such reorganization, and was characterized by the new psychology and the child study movement. As a result of these movements, the kindergarten itself was challenged both in its theory and practice and as a result was substantially modified.[8]

A new psychology based on the acceptance of the theory of evolution began to be taught in the leading universities in America shortly before the turn of the twentieth century. Psychological laboratories became common place in well-equipped educational schools and scientific research in psychology was carried out.

The Child Study Movement was moving along at full sail. It became a topic of interest to parents, teachers, interested citizens, teacher training institutes and universities. "The Child Study movement must be considered one of the epoch-making movements in the history of American education."[9]

The polemic between the varied kindergarten beliefs continued into the new century. To alleviate these tensions and to draft a statement on the present kindergarten position, a Committee of Fifteen was established in 1903. Susan Blow headed a committee of three who were to appoint additional members. Shortly after its formation, four more members were added making it a Committee of Nineteen. In 1907 the Committee presented their divergent opinions. By 1909 three separate reports were drafted: Liberal, Conservative and Compromise. Even through all this internal strife the number of kindergartens in the United States was increasing and an established pattern of kindergartens was being set.[10]

During the same period, the American school system, seeking to become more "democratic," was passing compulsory attendance laws, which would eventually restructure the whole educational system. Cremin emphatically stated, "Had there never been a progressive movement, had there been no social settlements, municipal reform associations, country life commissions, or immigrant aid societies, no William James, Stanley Hall, Edward Thorndike, or John Dewey, the mere fact of compulsory attendance would have changed the American school."[11]

The years just prior to the First World War were marked by a diversity of educational experiments and "a truly dazzling collection of pedagogical luminaries."[12] James Earl Russell, Dean-Elect of Teachers College, Columbia University had assembled many renowned leaders there. They included: Paul Monroe, pioneer in the field of American educational history; Edward Thorndike, who led in the field of educational psychology; John Dewey, educational reformer; William H. Kilpatrick, disciple and interpreter of Dewey; Patty Smith Hill, kindergarten leader, and others distinguished in the field of education.[13] These were the leaders in American education with whom the Montessori Method came face to face during the initial introduction of her method into the United States. Kilpatrick would contribute much to the Montessori debate later on.

S.S. McClure's magazine is generally credited with introducing Montessori to the American public in May 1911. McClure has been described by his biographer and others as a "genius;" "a geyser of ideas, a sensitive barometer of the moods of the time he lived in, "a supernatural senser of what people felt and thought;" "a vibrant eager, indomitable personality that electrified even the experienced and the cynical." He has been called the man who "made 'muckraking' synonymous with the era."[14] Lyon depicted him as one of the greatest magazine editors this country ever produced.[15]

Academics had already begun to take notice of Montessori's early experiments almost a year and a half before the first article appeared in *McClure's Magazine*. In a series of articles beginning in December 1909 and continuing until June 1910, Jenny Merrill, Ph.D. introduced Dr. Montessori and her method to American primary teachers. Her first article in *The Kindergarten-Primary Magazine* (a journal, "Devoted to the child and to the Unity of Educational Theory and Practice from the Kindergarten Through the University") was entitled "A New Method in Infant Education." She wrote, "Recently an able woman physician, Dr. Med. Maria Montessori, Docente all'Universita di Roma, has modified the kindergarten methods to such an extent as to warrant the title of this article."[16] She described the method used as reported to her by Baroness Franchetti, and concluded, "As has been claimed for the kindergarten, its various occupations need to be seen in operation to be fully appreciated. Miss Peabody, we all know, went to Germany before she really apprehended the value of the kindergarten. So the Baroness Franchetti says the Montessori occupations need to be seen to be fully appreciated."[17]

In these articles, written in the midst of the kindergarten controversy, Merrill wrote, "Altogether it behooves us to be liberal, not dogmatic, and to listen to the tale with interest."[18] She described the reading and writing which Montessori had reintroduced into the curriculum, and commented, "It did seem that we had succeeded in cutting out the three R's, but Dr. Montessori has put them back in the infant school in Rome and we must convince our Italian friends of the error or let them convince us."[19]

It appears Dr. Merrill sided with Patty Smith Hill, who wished to change the status quo of the kindergarten. She asked all those concerned with the current condition of the kindergarten "to study it (the Montessori Method) for it contains admirable suggestions", and added, Comparison of methods is valuable."[20]

The final article in the series looked at the Montessori Method more critically than the previous ones and recommended once again that teachers and others interested in the kindergarten make an effort to see the Montessori schools in Italy for themselves.

Interest in the Montessori Method seems to have come from many sources. As noted, Merrill was introduced to it by Baroness Franchetti. Horatio Pollack reported that he visited Rome in 1911 when, "my attention was called to the matter by the reform Mayor of Rome, Ernesto Nathan, who had been interested in the experiments from the very first." Ann George, a primary teacher, received a letter from a friend in Italy telling her of the new Montessori system. She was so impressed that she went to Italy, where she met Dr. Montessori and visited some model schools. She returned with a copy of Montessori's book (still not translated into English) and a complete set of the didactic materials. She returned to Italy in the summer of 1910 and took an eight-month training course (given to Italian teachers) with Dr. Montessori.

In the spring of 1911, just prior to the publication of the *McClure's* article Professor Henry W. Holmes of Harvard University wrote to Montessori expressing interest in her book and his desire to see it translated into English. About this same time, American educators (possibly on the advice of Merrill) began to visit Montessori's school in Rome.

The news of Montessori's work in Italy eventually reached the ear of S.S. McClure in a round-about way. Mary L. Bisland, who was *McClure's* London representative for his magazine received information from a friend of hers. This friend, Josephine Tozier, had spoken with Montessori and visited her schools in Rome for about six months.

McClure's Magazine, unlike *The Kindergarten Primary Magazine* was principally for the lay public. McClure related the events that led to his introduction of the Montessori Method to the United States. "Frequently the magazine's biggest successes," he wrote, "were articles whose interest was generally doubted." He admitted his articles on the Montessori Method fell into this category.[21]

Tozier was commissioned by McClure to write an article on the Montessori Method for his magazine. All articles of import were always submitted to people with expertise in the given field before publication. Tozier's article went through the same process. First, it was compared to the then-untranslated version of Montessori's book to determine if it depicted her theories accurately and then read by several authorities on kindergartens in the United States. As could be expected, "these experts . . . greatly differed in their estimates of Montessori's methods. Some of them were very antagonistic in their attitude," and wrote, "there was nothing new about her method."[22] McClure risked publishing it anyway.

The first article appeared in May 1911. It began with background material on the source of Montessori ideas and when and how the Children's Houses were organized, and then immediately reported, "The most conspicuous of Maria Montessori's triumphs is that of teaching quite young children, without putting the smallest strain upon their faculties, first to write and then to read." She included a photograph of a young child writing on the blackboard with the following caption under it: "ONE OF MARIA MONTESSORI'S PUPILS WRITING FROM DICTATION AT THE BLACKBOARD. THE AVERAGE CHILD OF FOUR LEARNS TO WRITE IN SIX WEEKS BY THE MONTESSORI METHOD."[23] This caption seems to be what fascinated so many of the readers.

Tozier then discussed Montessori's sensorial activities. Her auto-education and didactic apparatus was also described and pictured. Tozier detailed the practical life activities in which "Children of Three Learn to Tie Bows, Knots and to Fasten Buttons and Clasps."[24]

In this very complete article, Tozier told how children learned to spell, do arithmetic and play the "silence" game. The article returned to the early age at which children write, devoting an additional four pages to it, and concluded with expectations for the method to spread beyond Rome and Italy.

These expectations were realized immediately. McClure's office was deluged with letters of inquiry as was Montessori herself, in Rome. McClure concluded, "It seemed as if people everywhere had been waiting for her message."[25]

On Anne George's return to the United States, less than six months after the first article appeared in *McClure's Magazine*, she opened the first Montessori school in America in Tarrytown, New York, under the auspices of Mr. Frank A. Vanderlip and several of his friends.[26] She reported, "This school, unlike Montessori's first school in Rome, drew its students "from cultured families, whose greatest ambition it was to give their children everything possible in the way of education and rational enjoyment."[27] George said, "It was not, however, until after the publication of the article in *McClure's Magazine* that Dr. Montessori was able to realize that the interest already shown by individuals was indicative of the general readiness in the United States for the ideas upon which her work was based.

In October, 1911, *McClure's Magazine* printed examples of the many letters received and informed its readers that Dr. Montessori's book was soon to be published and promised to run a series of articles describing the method in greater detail.

The excitement generated by the new education in Rome piqued the interest of William Heard Kilpatrick, who was just beginning his teaching career at Teachers College, Columbia University. He would later be labeled by one of his biographers as, "the greatest teacher of his generation."[28]

A more recent biographer elaborated on Kilpatrick's state of mind around the time of the translation of *The Montessori Method* into English in 1912. He wrote that Kilpatrick was "not satisfied with the subordinate place at Teachers College, not satisfied that he lived away from the south, and not satisfied that he did not have a real home of his own."[29] While in the throes of this dissatisfaction, Kilpatrick read *The Montessori Method.* He speculated there might be some value to her method, but remained unconvinced. He wrote he was "reasonably sure that we cannot use it just so in America."[30] Some of her ideas seemed good while he questioned many others.

By April 1912, he had arranged to travel to Italy to observe the Montessori Method firsthand. On May 18, 1912, undeterred by the sinking of the Titanic, he and two colleagues sailed to Italy. None of them spoke Italian, although they had purchased a used copy of an Italian dictionary.

On June 4, they met with Montessori. One of the first topics, which came up, was her didactic equipment and who represented her financial interests in America. They also talked about other features of her method with which Kilpatrick disagreed in theory. Then some major misunderstanding appears to have transpired between the interpreter and Montessori's guests. Kilpatrick suggested that someone "had tried to queer our visit" and there were "crooked dealings" going on. The interview was concluded on an unsatisfactory note, although Montessori did give them passes to see other schools of hers.[31] He visited a number of her schools, most of which in his diary he expressed surprise at how well run they were and how happy the children were.[32] The team spent a little more than a week observing the schools before leaving for sightseeing throughout Italy and other parts of Europe. Kilpatrick seemed convinced that the method had nothing very new to offer American education.

Although critical of her ideas he did not pass up the opportunity to capitalize on the high level of interest in Montessori in this country. He presented innumerable lectures in the Midwest and the northeast. He, as well as others, was impressed with the audiences' acceptance of his ideas. He wrote, "I seem to carry the crowd with me."[33] In four years he rose from doctoral student to well-received lecturer. Later he would be dubbed the "million dollar professor," as he brought that much tuition to Teachers College, Columbia University.

By December 1911, *McClure's Magazine* reported that Montessori schools had already opened in New York and Boston and in response to the clamor for instruction, Montessori would give a course for teachers that winter. It also noted the manufacturer (House of Childhood) hoped to have the didactic apparatus ready for parents and teachers by the beginning of the year (1912).

The Montessori Method, the English translation of *Il Metodo della Pedagogia Scientifica applicato all'Educazione infantile nelle Case dei Bambini*, appeared in April, 1912 and the first edition of 5,000 copies sold out in four days. Immediately after this publication, *McClure's Magazine* published a newly written article by Montessori, herself, describing her method. In the early spring of the same year the Montessori American Committee was formed. Anne E. George, S.S. McClure and a few others hoped this group would serve to initiate the first training school in New York. Petty squabbling and personality conflicts within this committee and Montessori arose but finally the first International Training Course was organized in Rome. More than one hundred pupils from various countries enrolled for this course. The greatest representation was from the United States with sixty-seven students.

Mabel Bell (the wife of Alexander Graham Bell) was one of the many Americans who took a liking to the Montessori Method. In the summer of 1912, she opened a school in Beinn Bhreagh (near Baddeck, Nova Scotia) for her grandchildren and a few local children under the direction of Roberta

Fletcher. Because of what appeared to be a success, she began a new school in her home in Washington, D. C. in October, 1912. This school was headed by the aforementioned Anne E. George and Roberta Fletcher. This school operated from October, 1912 until April, 1913 when with strong urging from parents she agreed to open a permanent Montessori school in Washington.

This display of enthusiasm by the parents and the move to establish a permanent school in Washington led to the formation of the Montessori Educational Association, organized in 1913 and incorporated under the laws of Washington, D. C. Mabel Bell was elected first president.

She and the Montessori Educational Association were initially recognized by Dr. Montessori as a means for the dissemination of Montessori's ideas in America. Bell spoke on Montessori's behalf to the Mother's Club in the Washington area and by mid-1914 counted seven hundred members in her Association. Aware of the need to spread Montessori's educational ideas, she started a news *Bulletin.* The first *Bulletin* of the Montessori Educational Association lists the Aims of the Association: The Association stands pledged to spread the educational principles called the Montessori Method—

- By maintaining a central bureau where accurate information on Montessori matters may be obtained
- By keeping Dr. Montessori and all interested in this method in touch with each other through the Bulletin
- By supporting a Free Montessori School"
- By adding the establishment of similar schools
- By inducing educators and scientists to study the method
- By assisting Dr. Montessori to found an International Institute for training and experiment
- By aiding her to continue the development of the method.[34]

The first Free School was opened in Friendship House in Washington, D.C. on November 24, 1913. The second free demonstration school was started by the New York chapter in September, 1914, in the New Open Stair Tenement on Seventy-Seventh Street.[35]

Meanwhile, other Montessori societies were being formed. On May 24, 1913 the New England Montessori Association was started with seventy-five members from Canada and every state in New England except New Hampshire. Ellis reported "all shades of opinion are represented in the Association from radical Montessorians, who would abolish kindergartens, to those who believe in combining the two systems by using the Montessori material at a stated time in the regular kindergarten program."[36]

Other groups were holding informal meetings on the Montessori method while at least one unauthorized course of lectures by Myron Scudder was being conducted in New York City. Frances Haskell, director of the kindergarten of the first public Montessori class in Maine took this course which was described as the "most comprehensive course offered by anyone outside of Rome.[37]

Dr. Montessori recognized no other course but her own as valid. She went to some lengths to insure that only her course in Rome be recognized. She stated this in a letter to the *New York Times*. Approximately a year later, Montessori wrote another letter to another newspaper, *The London Times*, again protesting a non-authorized exposition of her ideas. This time it was about a book by Dorothy Canfield Fisher purported to have been written on Montessori's request. Montessori wrote, "I have not deputed—and do not propose to depute—to others the work of a practical popular explanation of my method, as I have taken great pains to do this myself. I hope my system will not be held responsible for any want of success that may arise out of the use of other books."[38]

Montessori's students had urged her to come to America. The Montessori Educational Association along with other friends of hers had asked her to come to the United States to visit the American schools and to lecture. She consistently refused. She was giving training courses in Rome and had prepared some films showing her children at work with the Montessori Method.

Because of financial difficulties arising from bad investments, S.S. McClure had been forced to sell his magazine. In 1913, he was out of a job and was just beginning a lecture tour around the country when he decided to see if he could convince Dr. Montessori to come to America to launch a lecture series for him which would feature her method and the film she had produced.

McClure's biographer wrote, "McClure traveled to Rome in the fall of 1913 to broach and subsequently clinch the deal. In the view of the Dottoressa, grateful for the attention given her work in *McClure's Magazine*, S.S. was a rich and powerful protector who could do no wrong."[39]

In his first letter to his wife from Rome, McClure wrote that Montessori herself owned the world rights to the moving pictures, and added, "I think it will be a money-maker." He told her that Montessori still had trust in him, and of the possibility of her coming to America to help launch the lecture series.[40]

Three days later, McClure indicates if Keedick (the manager) could guarantee expenses plus $1000 for Montessori and a teacher, Montessori would consider coming to America to give some lectures. He related his plan, "I am after the world rights on moving pictures of her schools and work, exclusive for a term of years, and the lecture rights in the English-speaking world."[41]

By the next day, McClure had secured the moving picture rights for North America and had arranged for Montessori to spend the month of December 1913 in America under Keedick's management. McClure was to get half of the profits from her public appearances. He wrote he was almost sure Keedick and he would make a good deal of money on her talks during December. McClure told his wife that Montessori knows about the loss of his magazine but has still retained her faith in him and added a cautionary note that the lectures must be written under her supervision.

The contract gave him the exclusive North American rights to the moving pictures. He agreed to pay the cost of the negative, pay 10% profit on lectures he delivered and 25% profits from marketing the films elsewhere in North America to Montessori. Dr. Montessori would receive 60% of the net profit of her lectures or at least $800 to be given to her immediately.[42]

The Montessori Educational Association prepared the way for Montessori's arrival. They announced her decision to come to the United States and to deliver twelve lectures. The first lecture was given to the passengers on board the *Cincinnati* enroute to America.

A reception was arranged for her in Washington. Four hundred people attended a dinner given at the house of Dr. and Mrs. Alexander Graham Bell on December 6, 1913. Some who attended were: Margaret Wilson, daughter of President Wilson, S. S. McClure, the French Ambassador; the Bishop of Washington; Minister of Peru, Secretaries of the Navy and Commerce, the Board of Education; Commissioner of Education; and many foreign ministers and dignitaries.[43]

On December 9 (six days after her arrival) Montessori lectured in New York's Carnegie Hall. Over 1,000 persons were turned away. It was arranged for her to deliver a second lecture there on December 15. The lectures were in Italian with Anne E. George translating them into English.

Montessori reported that she found the schools in America faithful to her method. After a successful lecture tour she left the United States at the end of December, 1913. Using the recent renewal of interest, she announced another international training course in Rome to be held from February 23 to June 30, 1914. Fifteen countries were represented at this course. Even though it was announced quite late, there were still forty-five American students enrolled.[44]

In the meantime, after Montessori had left the country, McClure continued his lecture series using the film rights he had acquired from her. Lyon described what happened, "behind the scenes there had been an unseemly scramble to exploit the Dottoressa, her Method, her apparatus, and everything else involved. McClure had scrambled with the others."

McClure claimed his motives were strictly altruistic, but in reality he was realizing a profit from her film and his lectures on her method. He had pocketed twenty per cent of the net proceeds of their joint tour (she got sixty per cent and Lee Keedick, the manager, got the other twenty). His biographer insisted, "Never had he been dishonest; but he had been naive, which, in the circumstances, was worse"[45]

Since Montessori was not willing to let anyone adapt or amplify her method and recognized only the International training course in Rome as valid, the Montessori Educational Association attempted to get Montessori to come back to America to give a training course. McClure, too, was interested in having Montessori give another course of lectures in the United States.

In April 1914, he sent his brother Robert, who had previously looked after his interests at the *McClure Magazine* syndicate in London, to Rome to speak to Montessori about this. Neither one of them expected the cold reception he received. Robert wrote to his brother, "I cannot help thinking someone in America has been poisining (sic) her mind and that influence together with this distrustful attitude of her entourage in Rome has made her thoroughly dissatisfied with her arrangement with you."[46]

After lengthy talks between the two, Montessori's demands included dissolving the Montessori Society of America and canceling all contracts, lectures, films, etc. She stipulated, "It was *her* enterprise, that if we had anything to do with it it was to be as her agent, everything must be submitted to and approved by her."[47] Montessori also told him that other people had offered to pay her to come to America to teach and she was able to handle this matter on her own.

When McClure realized matters had deteriorated too far, he returned the films and gave up the power of attorney which she had given to him. "Four months of exhausting work had netted him four hundred and ninety-two dollars and ninety-nine cents.[48]

On May 31, 1914, the *New York Times* reported the suicide the previous Friday, May 29, of Robert B. McClure in his home in Yonkers, New York. The article said he had been "ill and melancholy."[49] S.S. McClure's biographer reasserted the idea that the suicide was a result of illness and alcoholism, but added, "S.S., in his grief, could only recall that his last words to Robert had been spoken in anger because of a disagreement provoked by the Montessori tour."[50]

Gilbert H. Grosvenor, son-in-law of Mabel Bell and editor of the *National Geographic* wrote a very telling letter to his mother-in-law in reference to Montessori coming to America. He thought it would be best if Montessori remained in Italy and referred to her as a woman of "peculiar disposition." His letter continued, "She seems to lack the faculty of knowing who her friends are. We all know Mr. McClure's weaknesses, but I think his promotion of Madame Montessori and her ideas was entirely altruistic. She owes her entire success to him, and yet, because she thought he ought to have sent her $100 more . . . she writes him a most insulting letter and discontinues dealings with him." Montessori, he wrote, realized a net profit of $3600 which included the expenses of a maid. He then advised his mother-in-law to retire as President of the Association and added, "The situation will be very different when Montessori reaches America. She will be then the whole movement in America, and I am afraid there may be unpleasantness. Anyway you would be worried to death over her idiosyncrasies and her utter lack of responsibility."[51]

Montessori did come to America again but neither McClure nor the Montessori Educational Association sponsored her. The National Education Association and one of Dr. Montessori's pupils Catherine Moore of Los Angeles, California convinced her to come to the United States for the Panama Pacific International Exposition.

When it was learned that Montessori was returning to the United States for the Exposition, Mabel Bell wrote to the Smithsonian Institute in Washington asking them to give a public reception there for Dr. Montessori. Her request was turned down because she was told that the Board of Regents would not consider primary education.

During her stay in California, the Panama Pacific International Exposition through its Department of Education arranged to have Montessori give a training course at the Exposition for certification in America. The regular course was opened on August 1, 1915 in San Francisco and ran until November 30th, but some students were allowed to begin the course July 1st in San Diego and complete it in San Francisco by the end of October. "The principal object for organizing this course in connection with the Panama Pacific International Exposition is to afford an opportunity for thorough and critical study of this method of child training by leading educators who will gather in San Francisco during the summer."[52] A model classroom which could be seen through glass partitions was set up. These classes were directed by Helen Parkhurst, a former student of Montessori's (later originator of the Dalton Plan).

While Montessori was in California, the Montessori Educational Association attempted to establish more amicable relations between them and Dr. Montessori. Bailey Willis, Bell's representative, found Montessori "was sincerely anxious about the misuses of her name, the purity of her method. She repeatedly said she did not want the association to dissolve."[53]

Willis was given a copy of the "General Regulations for the Formation of An Authorized Montessori Society." This memorandum established that all teachers must have taken only Montessori's training course from the year 1913 on. It also set up a "Program for Propaganda." Although this term has negative connotations today, and some of the clauses display a sense of territorialism, the intent of the document was to protect the name and method of Montessori and to disseminate the method to the broadest base possible. It read as follows:

> The society should at once seek to have among its members lawyers, that they may study the legal questions relative
>
> 1. To the legal defense of the Method, of the name Montessori and of the rights of the graduates in order that no school or society may assume the name of Montessori without authorization.
> 2. For the defense of the method in each locality according to the laws of that particular state.
>
> It shall seek to have journalists or better still editors who will be ready to lend their assistance in a just and righteous propaganda.
>
> It shall endeavor to have businessmen among its members that they may study and learn what are the best means, from an economic and social standpoint, of diffusing the practice of the method.
>
> It shall endeavor to interest in the Montessori Method people prominent in the fields of science, letters, art, and above all local authorities in the educational and political world.

MEANS OF PROPAGANDA

The authorized means of propaganda of the regular societies are: Public lecturers, benefits, popular meetings, regular visiting days in the schools so that the method may be seen in operation, and articles for the papers.[54]

The stipulation in the agreement which insisted upon teachers being certified after 1913 seems to have been directed specifically against Anne George who had received her training prior to that date. Other points appeared to be aimed at the Montessori Educational Association, in particular. However, the Bells wanted a definite statement from Montessori herself, not inferences.

As early as September 29, 1915 there was talk of the Montessori Educational Association dissolving, however they were concerned about their life members and felt the Association had made inroads into the movement in America and any disharmony between the Montessori Educational Association and Dr. Montessori herself, would be liable to injure the Montessori movement in America.[55]

Montessori remained in America until December 5, 1915 when her father suddenly died and she went back to Italy.

In January of 1916, the National Montessori Promotion Fund was formed with Dr. Montessori as President. Helen Parkhurst was put in charge in New York. After three months, Mabel Bell, as President of the Montessori Educational Association, still had not received any official notice of this organization from Helen Parkhurst who was corresponding secretary of the newly organized fund.

Anne George, however, who the Montessori Educational Association had sent to Spain to try to clarify matters with Montessori, reported she was received well by Montessori and that it was Montessori's wish for both organizations to continue to function.[56]

Bell and the Montessori Educational Association found that the two groups had similar purposes. Additionally, the National Montessori Promotion Fund had more money, and was in closer touch with Montessori. They, therefore, decided to dissolve their organization.

Although, the Bells worried this friction might cause the movement to suffer, the statistics provided by the National Montessori Promotion Fund in 1917 do not appear to have had this immediate effect. For the school year 1916–1917, there were one hundred and four recognized Montessori schools in twenty-two states.[57]

A little more than a year after the inception of the National Montessori Promotion Fund, Helen Parkhurst considered splitting it into two groups— an east and a west division because the west was not supporting the Promotion Fund. Shortly thereafter, Bell received a letter from the National Montessori Promotion Fund informing her that their job was done and they were disassociating themselves from the organization. Parkhurst then left Montessori and began working on her own educational plan which would later be known as the Dalton Plan.

Americans were not the only ones interested in this innovation in education. Montessori schools were being started in England, the Netherlands, Ireland, South America, Greece, Spain and other countries. In order to ensure that the schools conformed to her ideals and principles, Montessori established the Association Montessori Internationale (AMI) in 1929. She was its first president and remained so until her death when she passed it on to Mario Montessori in her will.

Although the number of schools continued to grow throughout Europe and other parts of the world, the Montessori movement in America by the second decade of the twentieth century had reached its peak and was on the decline. Some schools still remained in the United States but for all intents and purposes the movement became dormant.

For years, Montessori had intuitively utilized many of the leadership skills that women today are rediscovering. It is important to explore why her approach to change broke down and a flourishing educational movement waned at the height of its expansion.

Montessori was introduced to America during a period when the American kindergarten was in the midst of turmoil. The well-defined Froebelian kindergarten was being challenged and proponents on both sides were emotional and arguments were heated. The liberals were trying to break free from the rigidity of a system that had become dogma after Froebel's death. Were they going to substitute another rigid system as desired by Montessori?

Montessori began her experiments with a series of hypotheses. She did not prescribe a methodology of education but rather a method of observation. In Italy, the Montessori Method relied heavily on the combination of physical anthropology and pedagogy. The physical anthropology was left behind when the Montessori Method came to America. The new psychology in America replaced physical anthropology. Her tentative hypotheses were soon translated into dogma. Kindergarten practitioners were willing to accept new ideas and materials, but not uncritically. Nor were they willing to exchange one set of dogma for another. Montessori insisted on a "pure" system. This purity was wished for but even the Montessori societies in the United States were not committed to this preciseness.[58]

Other writers have attributed the publication of Kilpatrick's slim book, consisting of only seventy-two pages, *The Montessori System Examined* with the demise of the movement in America. Although he thought her idea of auto-education was a good plan, Kilpatrick criticized Montessori's other ideas as being fifty years behind the times. He said her ideas were not original and were not valid in terms of present theoretical beliefs, and made the claim that children were beginning reading and writing at too young an age. He chastised her for the lack of play in her program.

Campbell wrote, "The book circulated among those who had the influence and power to really accept or reject Montessori. For already Teachers College was becoming the most influential teacher-training institute in the country and its graduates were holding high positions of control where policy and doctrine were set.[59]

From his lectern at Teachers College with an audience of approximately 35,000 students, Kilpatrick would deride the Montessori Method of education and its unscientific claims of its benefits for the American educational system. Whitescarver and Cossentino pointed out that although current research in cognition and brain research corroborate Montessori's claims, "Kilpatrick's "denunciations reached other 'teachers of teachers' in the newly created departments and schools of education in the colleges and universities of the United States." They added cogently, "professors of education were not about to wholeheartedly support the 'unscientific' claims, at least in their view, of a female from another country."[60]

Hunt believed that another reason the teachers did not accept Montessori is their desire "for an orderly classroom and for control of the educational process."[61] The Froebel kindergarten is teacher-centered whereas in the Montessori classroom the role of the teacher is limited to that of observer/helper. This demotion from the centerpiece of the classroom was irritating to many teachers. Montessori, who began by insisting the teacher observe the child, fell into the pattern of permitting the teacher to observe only her method of training. American teachers rejected this acceptance of a package deal.

Many believed the most important doctrine of interpreting educational reform movements in the United States was to understand the belief of Americans in the inevitability of progress and the major role the schools play in achieving this goal.[62] Americans looked to education and children for the hopes of bettering society. The government, too, placed this faith in the importance of the child. In 1909, just prior to the introduction of Montessori to America, the first White House Conference on children was held. Reports of Montessori's success in Italy made her methods appear to many of the most progressive-minded as the fastest route to basic reform.

Some educators had begun to suggest that Montessori's concept of Houses of Childhood (Casa dei Bambini) with their all day care of children was an excellent feature of her method. Montessori was even quoted in *Life* as saying, "We believe in taking the baby away from his or her mother just as soon as the child is born. That is because (t) he mother does not know how to care for her offspring. Parents require much training before they are to be trusted."[63]

If people saw education as the prime mover and the Montessori system as the fastest way to reform education why did the attitude of Americans suddenly change? For taxpayers the notion of extending the age for schooling down to three years (and maybe even to birth) looked like a highly unnecessary addition to the burden of school taxes. It appeared to some as an intrusion on the functions and rights of the family.

Montessori did not apply some of the basic principles of leadership and change which feminist organizations understand now, social change is cooperative not hierarchical. It must make incremental changes in the social fabric of the nation in order to be successful. There must be an understanding of the social climate of the recipient nation, which may be experiencing change concurrently.

When Montessori made her entrance on the American scene the country was committed to Dewey's concept of "learning by doing." This dovetailed very nicely with her principles. By the mid-teens and early twenties, however, "the climate changed, becoming preoccupied with the child's social and emotional adjustment and his relationship to the group."[64] Montessori was not in tune with this social shift. She was still teaching the theories of past scientists, and, according to the American media, propounding her belief in the intellectual development of the child. This, coupled with her inferences of usurping the function of the family, may have been one of the precipitating factors in the demise of the Montessori movement in the United States.

Between 1916 and 1918, Montessori divided her time between Catalonia, Spain and the United States. Mario Montessori said that one reason for the decline of the Montessori movement in America was "Dr. Montessori hated war and therefore made her headquarters in neutralist Spain when America joined the First World War."[65] He did not elaborate on this idea. He seemed to imply the absence of the leader from the scene. Standing supports this implication, "It would be interesting to speculate what might have happened if Montessori had decided to stay and work on the other side of the Atlantic (United States), concluding, "Certainly the history of the Montessori movement in America would have been very different."[66]

Hillyer carried this thought one step further. He made the point that, "Any idealistic system, no matter how impractical or even false in premises in the hands of its originator and his immediate disciples will show worthy results, for the divine fire of even a false prophet will inspire those in contact with it, but such a system when removed from the personality of its source will cease to bear the same fruit"[67]

While Montessori did not remove herself from the American scene, she alienated herself from many of the people who had worked tirelessly to bring her message to the United States. In her work on behalf of children with special needs, her peace efforts and her campaign for women's rights and suffrage, Montessori viewed power as energy, not control. When it came to her method of education, she insisted upon strict adherence to all aspects as taught only by her. One can speculate that she believed her method as a total package could bring liberty and freedom to all children and peace to the world or perhaps she viewed this as a lucrative commercial venture to replace the medical career she had sacrificed in order to disseminate her educational ideas around the world. Perhaps it was a combination of these two competing convictions.

Early in her career, at the International Women's Congress in Berlin, Montessori discovered the power of the press. Before the publication of her first book, *The Montessori Method*, in English she had already agreed to the articles which were published in *McClure's Magazine* and accepted his offer to come to America for a series of lectures in the United States utilizing a movie showing the workings of her schools which she had produced for publicity purposes,. Other approaches she utilized to bring attention to her newly discovered method were speaking at many conferences, publishing and granting interviews to many journals. These strategies and others were highlighted in her program of propaganda for the dissemination of her method into society.

In spite of all of her efforts to communicate her ideas, there is always a possibility with any new idea that there will be an intangible loss in translation from the author to the reader. Montessori's chances for this misinterpretation were two-fold: 1) the inevitable difference of understanding and 2) the actual translation from one language to another.[68] These inherent problems of translation, combined with external circumstances, may have led to various interpretations of Montessori's work. Lightner Witmer reported that Montessori had "not given an hour of instruction in her method to the swarms of American teachers" but she had "consented . . . to allow an assistant teacher of the experimental class in her own home to give them a few lectures on the work in the English language." [69]

Some people believed that the Montessori Method was only for children with disabilities. Others believed that only Catholic children could attend Montessori schools. *The New Republic* even printed a satirical article about one person who tried to open a Montessori school for Presidents.[70]

In addition to all of these external problems Montessori faced in establishing her method as an educational movement in America, she seems to have been her own worst enemy. She ignored one of the prime principles of leadership and change: members of a group must be empowered to work together toward a common goal to create change, transform institutions, and improve the quality of life.

Gilbert Grosvenor's admonition to Mabel Bell that Montessori did not know who her friends were seems to have been the case when she rejected the Montessori Educational Association in favor of setting up the National Montessori Promotion Fund in New York so that she might have personal control of it. The Montessori Educational Association, which had done much to spread the word of Montessori, promptly disbanded.

Montessori abruptly dismissed her friends when she felt they were not completely loyal to her. This is evident in the cold reception she gave Robert McClure, resulting in the return of her movie and other materials by S.S. McClure, one of the promoters of her method, even though he was making some money doing so.

She also rejected Anne George who according to the "Regulations for an Authorized Montessori Society," no longer qualified as a certified teacher because she had trained before the cut-off date.[71] Margaret Naumberg, another Montessori student, also did not get along well with her former teacher and attempted to set up a school in the Henry St. Settlement on Montessori principles. She later founded the Walden School.[72]

Helen Parkhurst also had a falling out with Montessori and set up her own school—the Dalton School. In defense of his mother, Mario Montessori related this incident, "After having given other courses in Los Angeles and San Diego, Dr. Montessori made a contract to establish a Montessori Training Center in New York where she intended to return periodically from Spain. She chose Miss Parkhurst to run it during her absences. . . During one of her (Montessori's) absences the contract was torn up and Dr. Montessori dismissed."[73]

Montessori's leadership or lack thereof, in terms of her physical presence and direct involvement with the movement, the lack of understanding of the social and educational climate of the United States or perhaps the disregard of it, her absolute need for control of her method, in spite of her inherent understanding of how change takes place, and her disregard for the people who were helping her, resulted in the disintegration of the Montessori movement on the American educational scene or the adoption of parts of it into existent early childhood practices.

The next chapter will explore the reintroduction of Montessori education to the United States and examine how Nancy McCormick Rambusch learned the leadership lessons that Montessori did not employ at the beginning of the twentieth century.

NOTES

1. John S. Brubacher, a *History of the Problems of Education*, (New York: McGraw Hill, 2nd edition, 1966), 385.
2. Ilse Forest, *Pre-School Education: A Historical and Critical Study*, (New York: The Macmillan Co., 1929), 293.
3. *Pre-School Education*, (Paris: UNESCO, 1963), 15.
4. http://nieer.org/resources/facts/index.php?, National Institute for Early Education Research, Rutgers State University, (2009). Downloaded, March 2, 2009. The NHES differentiates between categories of early education and care. Preschool or center-based early education care includes pre-kindergarten, day care centers, nursery schools and Head Start.
5. H.G. Good, *A History of Education,* (New York: The Macmillan Company, 1947), 472.
6. Adolph E. Meyer, *An Educational History of the American People*, (New York: McGraw Hill, 2nd edition, 1967), 310.
7. Nina C. Vandewalker, *The Kindergarten in American Education*, (New York: The Macmillan Company, 1917), 9–10. Vandewalker indicated that the dates given

are approximate because the movement differed radically in its origin and progress in each locality.

8. Ibid., 232–233.

9. Ibid., 239.

10. The latest census indicated there were more than 3.7 million American children attending either full or half-day kindergarten.

11. Lawrence A. Cremin, *The Transformation of the School,* (New York: Vintage Books, 1961), 128.

12. Ibid., 172.

13. Ibid., 172–173.

14. Robert Thacker, The Autobiography of S.S. McClure, (Lincoln: University of Nebraska Press, 1997), vii; Mark Sullivan, *The Education of an American,* (New York: Doubleday, Doran and Co., Inc., 1938), 194; Ida M. Tarbell, *All in a Day's Work: An Autobiography*, (New York: The Macmillan Co., 1939), 119 and 113.

15. Peter Lyon, *The Life and Times of S. S. McClure*, (New York: Charles Scribner's Sons, 1963).

16. Jenny B. Merrill, "A New Method in Infant Education," *The Kindergarten Primary Magazine*, (XXXIII, no.4, December, 1909): 106.

17. Ibid., 107.

18. Jenny B. Merrill, "A New Method in Infant Education," *The Kindergarten Primary Magazine*, (XXXIII, no.5): 143.

19. Ibid.

20. Ibid., 144.

21. S.S. McClure, *My Autobiography,* (New York: Frederick A. Stokes, Co., 1914), 251–253.

22. Ibid.

23. Josephine Tozier, "An Educational Wonder Worker—The Method of Maria Montessori," *McClure's Magazine*, (XXXVII, no.1, May 1911): 7.

24. Ibid., 11.

25. McClure, *My Autobiography*, 253.

26. Anne E. George, "The First Montessori School in America," *The American Montessori Society Bulletin*, (II, no. 2 and 3 (1964): 2.

27. Ibid.

28. Samuel Tenenbaum, *William Heard Kilpatrick: Trail Blazers in Education*, (New York: Harper and Brothers Publishers, 1951), 185.

29. John A. Beineke, *And there were giants in the land: The Life of William Heard Kilpatrick*, (New York: Peter Lang, 1998), 66.

30. William Heard Kilpatrick, Diary, April 7, 1912, Teachers College, Columbia University, Special Collections.

31. Kilpatrick, Diary, June 4, 1912.

32. Kilpatrick, Diary, June 8–12, 1912.

33. Kilpatrick, Diary, July 16, 1912.

34. *Bulletin of the Montessori Educational Association*, "Aims of the Association," (I, no.1, 1913).

35. Anne E. George, "The Montessori Movement in America," U.S. Commissioner of Education, *Report*, (Washington, D.C.: Printing Office, I, Chapter XV, 1914): 360.

36. Evelyn Ellis, "Minutes of the New England Montessori Association," (June 1913). McClure Manuscripts.

37. *Journal of Education*, "A Montessori Experiment in Maine," (77, March 20, 1913): 328.

38. Maria Montessori, "Letter," *New York Times*, (II, August 10, 1913) 10:6; "Letter," *London Educational Times Supplement*, (September 1, 1914): 151.

39. Lyon, *The Life and Times*, 350–351.

40. S.S. McClure, "Letter to His Wife," (November 7, 1913), McClure Manuscripts.

41. S.S. McClure, "Letter to His Wife," (November 10, 1913), McClure Manuscripts.

42. *The Memoranda of Agreements* entered into between the Dottoressa Maria Montessori of 5 Via Principessa Clotilde, Roma and S. S. McClure of 126 E. 24th St. New York City, (14th of November 1913), McClure Manuscripts.

43. *New York Times,* "Entertain Dr. Montessori," (iv, no.17, December 7, 1913): 6.

44. George, *Report,* 361.

45. Lyon, *The Life and Times*, 351.

46. Robert McClure, "Letter to S.S. McClure," (April 5, 1914), 1–7. McClure Manuscripts.

47. Ibid.

48. Lyon, *The Life and Times*, 352.

49. *New York Times*, "Find R.B. McClure Suicide in His Home," (May 31, 1914).

50. Lyon, *The Life and Times,* 352.

51. Gilbert H. Grosvenor, "Letter to Mabel Bell," (December 4, 1914). Bell Collection.

52. Panama Pacific International Exposition, (Berkeley, California, June 1915), Bell Collection.

53. Bailey Willis, "Letter," (n.d.), Bell Collection.

54. "General Regulations for the Formation of an Authorized Montessori Society," Bell Collection.

55. *Home Notes*, (September 29, 1915), 19–31. Bell Collection.

56. Mabel Bell, "Letter to Mrs. Pearson," (June 6, 1916). Bell Collection.

57. Mary Lorene Kerley Will, *Conditions Associated with the Rise and Decline of the Montessori Method of Kindergarten*, Unpublished doctoral dissertation, (Southern Illinois University, 1966). 37–38.

58. Evelyn Ellis, "Letter," 5, Bell Collection.

59. Donald N. Campbell, *A Critical Analysis of William Heard Kilpatrick's The Montessori System Examined,*" Unpublished doctoral dissertation, (University of Illinois at Urbana-Champaign, 1970), 27.

60. Keith Whitescarver and Jacqueline Cossentino, "Montessori and the Mainstream: A Century of Reform on the Margins," *Teachers College Record*, (110, 12, December 2008): 2579.

61. John McVicker Hunt, "Introduction," *The Montessori Method*, xvii.

62. Gilbert E .Donahue, "Montessori and American Education Literature: An Unfinished Chapter in the History of Ideas." (New York: American Montessori Society, 1964); Henry J. Perkinson, *The Imperfect Panacea: American Faith in Education, 1865–1965*, (New York: Random House, 1968).

63. *Life*, "N.B. Fathers and Mothers," (January 15, 1914):103.

64. Barbara Berger, "Researching Dottoressa Montessori," *The American Montessori Society Bulletin*, (VI, no.1, 1968):1.

65. Mario Montessori, "A Long Letter to Montessorians in America in Answer to Some of the Many Questions I Receive," (Amsterdam: M.J. Portielje, 1963), 4.

66. E.M. Standing, *Maria Montessori, Her Life and Work*, (New York: A Mentor-Omega Book, 1952), 64.

67. V. M. Hillyer, "Report of Lecture on the Montessori System," *Kindergarten Review,* (XXXIII, no. 4, December, 1912): 266.

68. Jacques Barzun and Henry F. Graff, *The Modern Researcher*, (New York: A. Harbinger Book, 1962), 301. It is questionable if Anne E. George, who learned Italian specifically to take Montessori's course and later did her translations, was the one most capable to do this.

69. Lightner Witmer, "A Caution on Montessori," *Journal of Education*, (6, July 4, 1912): 39.

70. Charles Merz, "Montessori for Presidents," *The New Republic*, (VIII, no. 95 August 26, 1916): 89.

71. This can be debated. A letter in the Bell collection proposed that this may not have been a direct attack on Miss George by Dr. Montessori but something written by one of Montessori's students, with the English language misunderstood by Montessori. Subsequently Montessori told Miss George that she wanted both societies; she supported only the National Montessori Promotion Fund.

72. Robert H. Beck, "Progressive Education and American Progressivism: Margaret Naumberg" *Teachers College Record*, (LX, no. 4, January, 1959):198–208.

73. Mario Montessori, "A Long Letter to Montessorians," 4.

Chapter Five

Montessori Education Returns as a Social Movement

How could I have known that majoring in Wednesday nights would change my life? Very shortly after my older daughter was born, I knew it was time to go back to school to complete the master's degree I had suspended a few years before. The first semester I took one class on Wednesday night, the best night for my babysitter. I loved it. In the summer I took two courses and by the time fall rolled around I was also taking two courses, both on Wednesday night. My final semester came very quickly and with two more courses left I enrolled in both of them on the same night. Yes, Wednesday night. I had no idea what Comparative Education would entail but I had the prerequisites and it was being offered on Wednesday night, so I signed up for it. Ursula Springer, the professor, would motivate me to not only want to know about educational systems throughout the world but also to continue my studies in the field. On my way to my doctoral degree, I sought a topic for my dissertation. Dr. Springer suggested Maria Montessori. As a comparative education major, I needed to live abroad to complete my research and since I had relatives who lived in Italy and a background in early childhood, Professor Springer thought Montessori would be ideal. But wasn't she Indian? Too embarrassed to reveal my confusion, I went to the library and found that Maria Montessori was indeed Italian and had made revolutionary changes in early childhood education. What a great subject.

In the summer of 1968 I packed up my two daughters, then five and two, and the three of us went to live in the outskirts of Rome. My relatives provided me with a woman to care for the children almost full time so I did not have to limit my research to Wednesday nights. Initially, I was going to compare the American and the Italian Montessori educational movements. I had learned a minimal amount of Italian before the trip and acquired more as I lived there, although I relied on English translations as much as possible. After my required stay abroad I returned home with some research completed, overwhelmed by the task ahead of me.

It was 1970, the centenary of Montessori's birth. There were celebrations everywhere. The AMI (Association Montessori Internationale) was holding its celebratory conference in Washington, D.C. From my research, I knew there was conflict between the American Montessori Society (AMS) and the AMI but unbeknownst to me I was soon to learn the real depth of this discord. I attended this conference hoping to learn more about the international aspect of Montessori education. The Montessori family was going to be there and they were scheduled to speak.

Providence, Fate, Luck? Maybe all of them. My life was to change one more time. Monday morning, anxious to get started I went for breakfast. I could hardly believe my eyes. Seated at the next table diagonally across from me sat Cleo Monson, the executive director of the American Montessori Society. What was she doing at an AMI conference? Taking a deep breath, I introduced myself. I could scarcely believe she asked me to join her for breakfast. By the end of breakfast, Cleo had not only agreed to allow me to do research at the American Montessori Society office but had asked me if I would be willing to go to Europe to photograph the Italian background of Montessori for a centennial celebration that AMS was planning. Would I be willing? I probably would have left immediately if I hadn't thought this conference would be so important for my dissertation.

I followed up on this chance meeting as soon as I returned home. Cajoling, laughing and using my under-developed Italian assisted me in obtaining funding from Alitalia Airlines and the AMS for travel to Chiaravalle (Montessori's birthplace), Rome (the birthplace of the first Casa dei Bambini) and Nordweg am Zee (Montessori's final resting place). The photographic essay that emerged from this trip was the beginning of my relationship with the AMS.

The following year proved to be busy and productive for me. Cleo introduced me to Nancy McCormick Rambusch and she opened her heart and the AMS files to me. My fascination with the behind-the-scenes drama rekindled the ever-burning embers of leadership and change which lived deep within me. I now had the research materials and the motivation to study the growth of the Montessori movement in the United States from the early period when Montessori herself was involved to its reintroduction by Nancy McCormick Rambusch.

It was time to speak to my doctoral advisor. Henry J. Perkinson is a scholar. It took little persuasion for him to accept the change in my dissertation topic. He understood the importance to the educational community of examining the role of leadership in the Montessori movement in a comparative perspective in America. I could follow my passion.

Montessori education at the turn of the twentieth century, with a few exceptions, had virtually vanished from the United States from the mid-1920's until the mid-1950's. There was no mention of Dr. Montessori in the *New York_Times* from 1917 until 1927, when notice was made of seventeen graduates from the Montessori Child Education Foundation Training School in New York City.[1]

Montessori schools continued to flourish in many other countries. Montessori's activities around the world were followed by the United States press from time to time. In 1949, 1950, and 1951, Dr. Montessori was nominated for the Nobel Peace Prize for furthering "international understanding through her educational work."[2] In 1952, her obituary was carried by many newspapers and magazines.

By mid-1950, nursery school education was a recognized institution in the United States. It evolved from institutions providing custodial service for working mothers during the war to ones organized for educational purposes. Because of the work of Jerome Bruner at Harvard, and 0.K. Moore at Rutgers there was increasing attention by the American public to the pre-school child's ability to learn. The child's potential for education became increasingly more understood and accepted.

Shortly after World War II this acceptance and complacency was replaced by vehement attacks on the schools. The basic premise of progressive education, that all children were capable of being educated was still accepted, but life adjustment education following on the heels of progressive education came under heavy criticism. Many educators feared the American educational system was moving in the wrong direction.[3] Leaders of life adjustment education were convinced the main goal of education should be preparation for the world of work. Their curriculum included personal hygiene, development of social skills and personality and inculcating industriousness.

Critics like Mortimer Smith appealed to parents to "indulge in some extensive critical examination, not only of the schools but of themselves," in order that they might realize the critical need for change in the structure of the present day education. He felt the main role of the schools should be intellectual and moral rather than concentrating on the whole child and basing the curriculum on the child's needs, interests, and abilities.[4]

Bell also had concrete recommendations for improving the schools. He suggested a restoration of basic training in the lower schools, greater emphasis on the 3Rs, a renewed stress on manners, a return to the rewards and punishment (promotion and non-promotion) system and a reverence for religion in the schools.[5] The theme of Bestor's work was that the public schools had become "Educational Wastelands." He wrote, "The schools exist to teach something, and that this something is the power to think." [6]

Educators, private citizens and local civic groups of all kinds seemed to have risen in unison to protest some aspect of public education. Caswell concluded, "At no time since the days of Horace Mann and Henry Barnard, in my opinion, has there been such widespread consideration of basic educational issues. This period will involve fateful educational decisions which might well result in major changes in the course of our educational development."[7]

At approximately the same time as Caswell was predicting major educational changes, Nancy McCormick Rambusch was telling Mario Montessori, head of the *Association Montessori Internationale* (AMI), that she was interested in establishing a "Montessori type" school in the United States. The account of her first school and the founding of Whitby school on September 29, 1958 in a Greenwich stable-carriage house can be found in Chapter Three.

Before this first school materialized, much groundwork had to be laid for the Montessori revival in America; before the name of Montessori became a familiar one to the American public there were many polemic encounters. The movement met up with many of the same issues in its renascence in America that it had experienced in its first appearance here. The controversy centered on the following issues: religious factors, cultural interpretations, teacher training, democratic representation and internal personality problems. Two major factors were very different in the second half of the century. The first was the academic climate of the late 1950s and, more importantly, the leadership and determination of Nancy McCormick Rambusch.

Changes in education can come very slowly but the anxiety aroused by the launching of the Russian Sputnik in 1957 resulted in a prompt response by the American government and the academic community for a rapid transformation of the educational system.

Nancy took full advantage of this climate and matched the anxiety of parents with the benefits of the Montessori system. She related the reasons for the resurgence of interest in the Montessori movement in the United States, "Some reasons are historical, and some reasons are hysterical. The historical reasons are precisely that we now know more about the importance of early years of child development." She quoted Dr. William Fowler, who "pointed out that in thirty years of research on techniques in improving children's learning, in terms of methodology, Montessori is the only name that stands out."[8]

"Hysterically," she wrote, "rather than historically, I would say that parents, understandably, are anxious to do the best for their children. They are extremely upset at the notion of leaving their children in the vestibule of life until the age of six." She continued, "This has happened before. At the beginning of the progressive education movement J. Stanley Cobb said: 'I see an army of mothers arising who want something other and better for their children.'" She added, "I think this is the same army only these are probably the grandchildren of these grandmothers. So this is sort of a normal development in the American educational system." [9]

When Nancy introduced Montessori education to the United States in 1958, she said, the pendulum had swung from the emphasis on life adjustment back to where "to live fully as a child was to use your intelligence."[10] This academic orientation was in keeping with Montessori's ideas.

A Company, Creative Playthings, had become interested in Montessori's didactic materials as early as 1954. In 1956, Nancy, who still kept in touch with Mario Montessori wrote to him about this interest. She told him of Creative Plaything's belief "that America is very ready for Montessori." She explained the two-fold interest of this company and their plan to set up a workshop for the demonstration of the material:

1. as a prestige measure, as they are in the forefront of well designed and significant school apparatus, not only for public and private schools but also for schools for the blind for emotionally disturbed and for mentally retarded children. And would like to acquaint American teachers with a completely integrated method.
2. as a commercial concern they are not able to be partisans of Montessori or any other method, but would be interested in acting as agents or possibly manufacturers of the materials.

Their idea is that if Montessori can be presented as a vital, living thing, the prejudices everywhere rampant and concerning the method will disappear and the climate will be prepared for some new efforts.

Nancy then presented her views on the value of such a demonstration. She wrote asking for his approval and told him she believed the workshop "would do more for Montessori in America to make her work known than 1,000 teachers like myself who would quietly attempt to affect a tiny fragment of the population."[11]Ada Montessori (wife of Mario Montessori) answered expressing interest in this device as a means to "pave the way for creating a real interest."[12]

Nancy pursued this and other avenues for reintroducing Montessori education to the United States. A Catholic herself, she employed her "psychic franchise" to gain the support of the Catholic community for the Montessori revival. It was her belief that the dissatisfaction with the existent education in the United States (recently intensified by the launching of the Russian Sputnik), coupled with the established pattern of paying for parochial education by these Catholic parents was the proper combination for the Montessori revival. So, most of her public addresses, lectures, writings and private contacts were directed to the Catholic audience.

As noted, the first article that Nancy wrote appeared in *Jubilee*, a Catholic magazine. It brought a flood of letters from parents who wanted to know if this system could be used in the United States. The article, similar in tone to the Josephine Tozier article in *McClure's Magazine*, described the rich, prepared environment for learning in a Montessori school, with one major difference. The *Jubilee* article stressed the religious aspects of the Montessori curriculum which was noticeably absent from the *McClure's* review. Nancy stated, "Religion is the core of the Montessori curriculum. Dr. Montessori devoted much thought to the most effective method of teaching religion to small children. She emphasized the presence in the small child of an acute sensitivity to religious matters, but she knew that religion must be taught in relation to what the child already knows of life."[13]

On November 24, 1958, an appeal was made to some prominent Catholics in Connecticut. A long letter was sent to some influential people in the Greenwich community. It outlined the concerns of Arthur Bestor and Rear Admiral Hyman Rickover about the life adjustment curriculum in the public schools. Whitby School was being proposed to "overcome this problem by giving the child a sound moral and intellectual foundation."

The letter explained, "The underlying philosophy of the school is that of Maria Montessori, whose influence has been widespread in Europe and Asia for the past half century. Montessori has proven that children are far more capable of intellectual achievement than they are generally credited to be."[14]

Many affluent, educated Catholics who were unhappy with the conditions in the Catholic parochial schools, yet were unwilling to send their children to public schools, responded. "They were attracted not only by the method's amazing academic results, but by its realistic, respectful, and deeply spiritual attitude toward the child."[15] Although Whitby was not officially a parochial school, religion was an integral part of the curriculum there. More than 10% of Whitby's students (65 pupils were enrolled at that time) were non-Catholics, and did not have to participate in religious instruction if they did not wish.[16] In one of the first published accounts of Whitby School which appeared in *Jubilee* there is a full page picture of Nancy instructing the young children in the meaning of the Holy Communion. "A large cross hanging over a communion altar in the classroom completed the visual."[17]

In April 1960, Nancy read a book review of the biography, *Maria Montessori: Her Life and Work*, by E.M Standing, by John J. McDermott in *Commonweal*. In this review, McDermott took notice of Nancy McCormick Rambusch's role in bringing Montessori education back to America and of her article in *Jubilee* magazine. In summarizing Standing's biography, McDermott noted that although the book was uncritical and sentimental, these deficiencies should not stand in the way of an intensive renewal of the study of the thought of this most challenging and original thinker.

Nancy knew she had to meet the author of this book review. Together, she thought, they would address the issue of cultural accommodation. At the time he was a Professor of Philosophy at City University/Queens College. Later she would write that he forced the AMS leadership to address just that question.

McDermott urged Montessorians to update Montessori's philosophy and make it relevant to the time and place in which it was being interpreted or reinterpreted. He believed the reason for the renewed interest in Montessori in America was a willingness to view Montessori's ideas in a new light, taking into consideration her developmental contributions to learning theory.

He was appointed by Nancy to present his theories to the teacher training classes. He presented a lecture every Friday. His concerns reached far beyond the manipulation of materials and classroom pedagogy. He was convinced the Montessori movement would remain just one of many social movements in America if it remained on the periphery as opposed to moving to the center of the culture. His task in teacher training became that of placing Montessori education into an American context, moving it beyond the parochial perspective of the parents who were interested solely in their own children and not in all the children of the nation. He continually expressed the need for egalitarianism, the necessity for studying the cultural pluralism of the country and for feeling what he called the "American pulse." He emphasized the idea that, "Any approach to education that attempts to speak about the child or learning for all time or in a way that precludes the burden of constant response to change at the behest of new data is an approach that runs afoul of this overall cultural acceptance."[18]

McDermott helped establish the framework for putting Montessori education into an American cultural context for the American Montessori Society. Guided by this view of Montessori as a social movement, the AMS rejected the teaching of Montessori's insights as dogma, which they said had been inspired by the original contact with the charismatic personality of Dr. Montessori. They determined that in order to meet this goal it was necessary to train teachers to meet American professional teacher-training standards, i.e., a college degree, courses in child development and in historical and philosophical foundations of American education. It was decided that everyone who trained to be a Montessori teacher must already be a college graduate so that in the future these teachers would have parity with other early childhood programs in the United States. McDermott believed it was necessary to introduce Montessori education into the teacher's colleges. He said it was the only way it would succeed. All of these ideas ran counter to the plans of Mario Montessori and his European organization.

Although McDermott was involved with the day-to-day teacher training problems and lectures, the vision which he held for Montessori education in America was always focused on the larger picture. After concluding that Montessori's insights on early childhood learning fit into the American cultural scheme, he believed the task was "to direct energies toward feasible points of contact with the needs of American culture so as to meet these problems head-on."[19]

He continually stressed the need to make Montessori education relevant to present problems and did not view Montessori education as a single solution to the problems in American education. He challenged the American Montessori Society to examine the ways in which growth and change occur in America. Of particular significance for the American scene, he believed, were the traditions of public education and the needs of an egalitarian-oriented society. He advised Nancy and the American Montessori Society to move beyond the tight-knit Catholic community. He foresaw an educational movement that would reach beyond private schools into the public school system. Nancy understood the possibilities of Montessori education as an educational and social movement.

A major obstacle, to this however, was the problem of teacher training. Dr. Montessori, throughout her life, insisted that her training course (in which Mario Montessori assisted) was the only valid course for training teachers. Therefore, at the time of her death, there were few recognized people accredited by AMI to train teachers. This was one of the factors which later became an issue between Nancy, the AMS and the AMI.

Early in their relationship, Nancy wrote to Mario Montessori to begin the process of teacher-training. She reported on the possibility of obtaining a foundation grant to set up a Montessori teacher-training institution in affiliation with Whitby. She told him how important it was to centralize the authority for Montessori teacher training in the United States, emphasizing the fact that her position as the official representative of AMI was important in obtaining the grant money.

Two months later, she received the following letter from Mario Montessori, General Director of AMI:

This is to certify that Mrs. Robert E. Rambusch of 33 Orchard Street, Cos Cob, Connecticut, U.S.A. has been appointed the representative of the Association Montessori Internationale for the U.S.A. with the special tasks of starting Montessori schools in the country, taking steps necessary to start a Montessori Society affiliated to the Association Montessori

Internationale and an institution or training teachers in the Montessori method.[20]

In a letter six months later, Nancy informed Mario Montessori of the formation of the American Montessori Society with its headquarters at Whitby School. She also related AMS's ideas for teacher training. AMS believed the teacher training program should be such that only students with university degrees could take it, otherwise Montessori education might be discredited as unworthy of consideration by serious-minded people.

By the end of February 1960, the American Montessori Society requested admission to the Association Montessori Internationale as a National Society. Nancy stated the aim of the American Montessori Society as, "the dissemination of the philosophical and pedagogical ideas of Dr. Montessori, the establishment of Montessori schools in America, and the creation of a Teacher Training Center, under the direction of A.M.I."[21]

Anxious to begin teacher training, she wrote to Mario advising him that Margaret Stephenson, of Great Britain, subject to AMI approval, was assisting in the organization of the teacher training, center. She was one of the few AMI approved teacher-trainers, who had been training teachers since 1946. In a follow-up letter to the official letter designating Nancy Rambusch as the American AMI representative, Mario had mentioned Margaret Stephenson as a possible teacher-trainer.[22]

Therefore, assuming Miss Stephenson would be acceptable to Mario Montessori and the AMI, Nancy arranged with the State Department for the official residency of Margaret Stephenson and Michele Pourtale, who was to be Stephenson's assistant in charge of the demonstration class. As the sponsor of these two individuals on the Exchange-Visitor Program, Nancy wrote to the United States Immigration and Naturalization Service requesting a two-year extension of their stay in order to carry out the objectives of the Montessori teacher training program.[23]

Almost nine months after sending her letter, Nancy, as president of the newly formed American Montessori Society, received a positive reply to her request for AMS to become a member of AMI with certain provisos: AMI retained the right to start other societies in the United States if it considered this to be necessary and AMS "will do all it can to spread the items we shall send for distribution and to make the movement known in your country as widely as possible. The affiliation fee is determined in agreement with each individual branch, but generally it consists of 10% of the Society's income to be sent directly to the Treasurer of the A.M.I."[24]

The first meeting of the incorporators of the AMS, Nancy McCormick Rambusch, Mary M. Begley and John R. Bermingham, was held on May

22, 1961. At this organizational meeting the Articles of Understanding were discussed and adopted and the directors of the corporation accepted.[25]

On August 5, 1961 Mario Montessori informed the AMI that Nancy McCormick Rambusch had requested that her power of personal representative of AMI to the United States be transferred to the American Montessori Society.[26]

For reasons that cannot be fully ascertained, six weeks later Mario Montessori was unhappy with the attempts by Whitby to arrange for visas for the teacher trainers and seemed to be looking elsewhere to start another Montessori society. I can find no evidence for Mr. Montessori's belief that Whitby and AMS were not trying to retain these two trainers at that time since this immigration problem had a direct relationship to the success or failure of the Montessori program. These teacher-trainers were needed for the training course which was in progress in Greenwich, Connecticut and they were the only AMI-accredited, English-speaking trainers.

Three months later, AMS was still working on this matter. An attorney was consulted for his legal advice concerning the immigration problem of these teachers. He explained the basic law, the Smith-Mundt Act, which had been in effect since 1948. It provided for reciprocal exchange of students, trainees, teachers, guest instructors, professors and leaders in fields of specialized knowledge and skills between the United States and other countries. Many countries had cancelled these reciprocal agreements because many visitors wanted to remain in America and the United States had granted them permission. It was, therefore, his opinion that a waiver would not be granted for these teachers to remain in the United States.[27] These communications continued for months with the result that Stephenson's visa was extended until March, 1963. Pourtale married an American removing the need for an extension of her visa.

In addition to teacher-trainer problems, the AMS was beginning to question what the relationship between AMS and AMI should be. They held an informal meeting just prior to Nancy leaving for Europe to formalize the tentative agreement, called the Articles of Understanding between AMI and AMS. She believed this agreement was necessary because it would permit AMS to take advantage of European Montessori teacher-training specialists who were in close contact with Mario Montessori until AMS was capable of training their own teachers.[28] AMS was also concerned that it could not prevent other Montessori groups from forming in the United States and that "in order to insure the quality of Montessori trained teachers and thus the proper growth of Montessori education, AMS must gain a franchise from AMI for teacher training."[29]

They also questioned the appointment of members of a Pedagogical Committee solely by Mario Montessori. Nancy said this problem could be handled in two ways; either to work for the appointment of people sympathetic to the AMS point of view and/or to "neutralize" the Pedagogical Committee by selecting a National Educational Advisory Board. She noted this would be permissible by the clause in the Articles of Understanding that said teacher training should reflect the United States teacher-training standards.[30] A recommendation was made for AMS obtain the franchise for teacher training and permission for AMS to produce Montessori materials. It was believed that AMI would agree to this since it received 10% of all tuition for teacher training and a 10% royalty on profits received from materials produced. Nancy went to Europe April 11–22, 1962 to sign the Articles of Understanding.

At the May 16, 1962 Board of Directors meeting, Nancy reported on the agreement she and Mario Montessori signed. She explained it was in simple form to allow for flexibility for the AMS because of its rapid growth. She related that AMI wanted 10% of the profit from the training program and possibly also from other activities sponsored by AMS.

During the preceding year, Nancy and the AMS Educational Advisory Board had formulated their view of the Montessori revival as a social movement. They had determined that to meet this goal it was necessary to train teachers to meet American professional teacher-training standards, i.e., a college degree, courses in child development and in historical and philosophical foundations of American education. These views were not shared by European Montessorians.

Stephenson approached a Washington group to discuss the possibility of AMS sponsoring a teacher-training course in Washington, D.C. In the middle of May, Nancy met with them to discuss the proposal. She described this meeting as one in which "the sentiments of the Washington group appeared oriented almost exclusively in the direction of Montessori training as 'mystical initiation,' and not professional formation," and expressed extreme dismay that in all the years since Maria Montessori had been training teachers there were only six people qualified, in the opinion of AMI, to train other teachers.[31] She concluded that a valid teacher training course must be established in line with American professional standards and also opted for the expression "pure" Montessori to be replaced with "objectively valid" Montessori as suggested by Mr. Frederic Ossorio of the AMS board.[32] Guided by their view of Montessori as a social movement, Nancy and the AMS rejected the teaching of Montessori's insights as dogma.

The first Montessori seminar was held in Greenwich, Connecticut in June, 1962. It was attended by representatives from the various local societies that had come into being in the past two years. At this time, the 1961–1962 graduates of the first American teacher-training course, disturbed by the rumors of tension and friction which had begun to be circulated about different AMS and AMI teacher training standards, approached Mario Montessori with their problems. Annoyed by this action, Nancy called a meeting just prior to the opening of the seminar to discuss their questions with both Mario Montessori and herself present.

At this meeting, Rambusch described how the AMS was formed and indicated that it had since grown to approximately forty members, thirteen schools and twenty-seven study groups. She explained that for a certain period of time the Board of the Montessori Society and the Board of Whitby School were identical because as directress of the Whitby School and President of the Montessori Society she found it efficient. The AMS, she told them, was a volunteer nonprofit, autonomous educational organization. Initially, this type of group is responsible to an appointed board, and then it elects a board that is more responsive to the wishes of its members.

Nancy then related her reasoning for requesting that her status as personal representative of AMI to the United States be turned over to the AMS. She told them, "We don't live in a culture where people function as personal representatives. We only send personal representatives to places like the Vatican where there is no constituted democratic government. As part of the American process, we tend to want an organization to replace the individual."[33]

Questions were raised from the floor about the representation of an American on the International Board of Directors, the legal structure and the bylaws of AMI. Mario answered that if he saw fit to put a capable American on the board he would, and that he selected (previously it had been Dr. Montessori and he) all members of the Pedagogical Committee, and that the Committee "can change from one moment to another the members of the Pedagogical Committee if we see that they are not functioning in the right way."[34]

The graduates pushed the issue further. The question was then asked as to where the complete authority existed in addition to the Pedagogical Committee. Mario responded that AMI could withdraw its recognition at any time if the AMI rules were not followed and another group could be formed. This answer did not satisfy the attendees who later in the seminar raised questions about democratic representation of the different geographic areas in the country. They also wanted to know who would vote, who would serve on the board and how they would be elected.

During the seminar, Nancy and Mario once again spoke to the graduates of the inherent problems of preserving the "pure" Montessori Method. The crux of the entire debate that followed between the two was a continuation of the intent of the AMS to insert Montessori ideas into American culture rather than maintain it as a distinct Montessori phenomenon, running parallel to the American educational scene. When this premise was accepted by Mario Montessori as valid, Nancy moved to the heart of the issue, which was total accommodation to the American educational picture, not changes in minor details.

Nancy told the graduates that with AMS functioning as a representative of the AMI, two points of view must be recognized. In order to preserve the integrity of the Montessori ideas, "There is an irreducible nucleus of insights that one transmits from culture to culture without diluting them or perverting them." And, in translating the Montessori insights or inserting these in a culture there are practical problems of that culture that must be faced. She stated that Mr. Montessori calls them the "essentials" and the "non-essentials" of the Montessori approach. The "essentials" are those without which it would not be Montessori while the "non-essentials" are all the cultural elements that enter into change.[35]

At that juncture, Mario Montessori said he felt that this point was not very clear and he would like to explain. He said there was an "impression that in each culture someone is going to try to transform the Montessori Method, that introducing certain facts of culture might bring situations of saying this it not the pure Montessori Method." He added this might be the case but then you have to distinguish.[36] He told a story of how a group of missionaries tried to use Montessori's exact method of serving meals with tables and forks. They failed, because in that country children ate on the floor with their hands and did not use tables and chairs and knives and forks as prescribed by Dr. Montessori. He said that Dr. Montessori replied "try to give them the responsibility and techniques of conducting exercises of practical life in their culture." Some changes are legitimate, he said. "But if it attacks essential, changes of depriving the child freedom, for instance, or trying to impose at a certain age things that are not there or trying to deprive the child certain experiences, then those changes are not allowed, then it is not legitimate."[37]

Nancy indicated that the change AMS desired was of a non-essential type. It had to do with the communication of some of the materials as a reflection of the culture. She gave them what she called practical examples, "the blessed phonogram booklets and the mathematical terminology which the AMI and the Pedagogical Committee directed be used by all English-speaking societies."[38] A discussion ensued as to the seventy different phonograms in English and to the competence of the Pedagogical Committee in judging the proper use of a language. Nancy contended the Committee could qualify as Montessorians but not as linguists. Mario insisted that the Pedagogical Committee must set standards and the final decision must be in the hands of the Pedagogical Committee of Montessorians. Nancy replied that it works if the child learns it.

The differences between British and American mathematical terminology was discussed, with Mario agreeing that the terminology of the country must be used. Nancy then stressed it went beyond the actual mathematical terminology, that it was part of the "business of relating the nucleus of ideas to the culture." She said this was a particular American problem because math and science were highly sensitive areas in American culture at that time. She added that the Pedagogical Committee, which was comprised of competent Montessorians, who were capable of judging the material for the validity of Montessori's ideas, comprised no Americans.[39]

Mario retorted, "I am at the head of the Pedagogical Committee of the whole world, automatically just because I am I. Any change on any proposed procedure must come back to us. I am at the head of the Pedagogical group of America and also of other countries." He added that the Pedagogical Committee would have the final decision as to whether or not it held to the integrity of Montessori.[40]

Nancy, who had visited almost every Montessori school in the country, then brought up a "typical American dilemma" which she found to be prevalent around the country: What if you do not accept religion? She mentioned one group whom she referred to as "humanists" who were irreligious and wanted to start a Montessori class. Another group said if one does not accept the spiritual nature of the child, he may not conduct a Montessori class. She suggested neither mention of the word secular or religious be used in the definition of the Montessori society. Mario responded that in the statutes of A.M.I. it says that "members can join irrespective of religion, race, etc. We cannot tie ourselves to any special religion." He added, "The Montessori method is like a medicine—there is no Catholic medicine." Then he threatened to withdraw if the AMS included these differences as essential.[41] Nancy agreed, but added that a pluralistic society must respect differences of belief.

She returned to her ongoing concern for standards in America and the insertion of Montessori's ideas into the American culture. She asked Mario about a mechanism for regulation of international teacher-training standards, and asserted in a country where taking care of children had professional status there was the problem of qualifications for teacher accreditation. She expressed her desire to be able to use Montessori effectively in the general American picture using standards that were yet to be evolved. She questioned him as to the astonishingly small number of people qualified to teach teachers and asked what program the AMI envisaged for training the teachers of teachers. Mario responded, "The original function of the Montessori society was to protect Dr. Montessori's work, so the only valid course was Dr. Montessori's and mine. As long as she was alive there was no problem." Now, he continued, there were people who had worked under Dr. Montessori or him whom he would guide, using Dr. Montessori's lectures, to be trainees.[42] The necessity for regulatory standards to prevent anyone from setting up a Montessori training school utilizing past unqualified Montessori trainees was discussed and Mario finally suggested setting up a screening board in order for a teacher to be recognized as capable of conducting a training course.

The focus at this seminar was an urgency to form a strong organization in order to make Montessori education succeed as a social movement and not be eclipsed as it had been previously. Robert Higgins, who chaired the June 7th meeting, explained it this way:

> It is my opinion that we have one more chance to make Montessori a success in this country. We are at the eleventh hour now. It is up to us now to make Montessori grow and be strong in this country. I think if we don't meet the challenge, if we don't this week form a strong national organization, we might as well resign ourselves to not have Montessori in this country, because at this moment we are not strong. At this moment we are twelve or thirteen schools that will decline, become semi-Montessori, then pseudo-Montessori, then not Montessori at all. So, we here, must either form a strong national organization in affiliation with the international society and go forward to further the Montessori movement, to make it grow, to make it be good, to keep it pure and to make it progress, to make it adapt itself to what the circumstances are. We here today are embarking on a policy of the most serious move in education in this country in this century.[43]

Professor Sally Cassidy spoke at this seminar too, emphasizing the factors needed to make Montessori a social movement. She indicated that every movement must find "its appropriate structure." Before institutionalization could take place, she said, enthusiasm for the young must be created. She said Americans like social movements and are willing to put in effort. The tasks involved would be setting up a dialogue, convincing people this type of education makes more sense, but cautioned there was the danger in thinking of Montessori as a single answer. She warned that Americans are very wary of single solutions.[44]

The recurring theme of Americanization played a prime role in this June, 1962 seminar. The seminar ended with the hope of forming a strong representative national organization and Mario Montessori professing solidarity with the aims of AMS as stated at the seminar.

On June 12, 1962, the American Montessori Society signed a five year agreement with the Association Montessori Internationale. The basic ideas of this agreement were: 1) AMS was sole representative of Montessori in

America. 2) AMS promised to disseminate Montessori's ideas. 3) AMS would set up and direct training programs. 4) AMS would offer employment to all AMI- certified teachers who wanted to conduct a program in the United States.

Further teacher-training problems arose shortly thereafter. The Pedagogical Committee met twice in June, 1962. At these meetings, the course content of the Montessori training course was outlined. It was decided to base this course on the 1947 lecture notes of Dr. Montessori and on her three texts, *The Discovery of the Child*, *The Secret of Childhood*, and *The Absorbent Mind*. As a minority of one, Nancy vigorously protested "that making only the Montessori portion mandatory in fact trained the teachers in a vacuum and ignored the advice and warnings of the professional educators good enough and interested enough to serve on the Educational Advisory Board."[45]

One educator advised including "the insights of developmental psychology and an appreciation by the teachers teaching in the United States of the philosophical, social and political foundations of American education." He added, "Any educational system must be housed in context. The context of the American Montessori school is 20th century America, in which new devices are constantly coming to the fore in the social sciences." He warned not incorporating this knowledge "would be a great mistake in judgment."[46]

In the midst of all of these teacher-training issues, Nancy and the AMS board encountered even more difficulties. The Whitby School board, most of whom were on the board of directors of AMS, held a meeting about one month after the AMS seminar in Greenwich. By that time, two members of the Whitby board had already resigned from the AMS board and two more were considering doing the same. At the meeting, it was pointed out if Whitby School were to "retain control of the AMS board as presently established, Whitby must provide the leadership for AMS; and conversely, if Whitby did not provide the leadership, it should not retain control.[47] Four days later, Philip Drake wrote to Nancy informing her that the Whitby School board would no longer delegate 11 members of the 20–member AMS Board of Directors.[48]

AMS, now more nationally representative, continued to press for the Americanization of Montessori's insights. At an Executive Board meeting, Nancy reported the idea of Margaret Loeffler and Lena Wickramaratne that, rather than re-orienting European teachers, they train American teachers themselves. Nancy volunteered to coordinate the courses and lecture on the American aspects of Montessori education.

In accordance with the provision in the agreement to set up teacher-training courses, Nancy met again with the Washington group, which had expressed an interest in setting up a training course. On July 12, 1962, the AMS received a letter reporting on this meeting and advising the board of the Washington group's surprise at the rumor of the possibility of the formation of a Montessori splinter group.[49] The Executive Committee voted a week later to establish a Montessori training course in Washington if they could have at least 75 paid applicants by August 3, 1962.[50]

AMS was running into many problems trying to get this movement off the ground. On the day of their board meeting they received a telegram from Mario Montessori indicating he was disturbed by the Whitby board resignations, uncertain if recognition for the AMS would continue and that he disapproved of the course planned by Nancy. The group was concerned about this telegram and much discussion followed about studying the AMS-AMI relationship in detail. Nancy said she would like to see this study include the effects of this relationship on teacher training because of the differences between European and American standards of education.

The next day, Nancy dictated a letter to Margaret Stephenson informing her that there would be no Montessori training course in Washington because only three people had registered in spite of her efforts to stimulate interest in the Washington area. This letter was followed twelve days later by a request for Stephenson's visa status and her willingness to work in the event that AMS could start a training course and obtain the funds to pay her salary.

On September 5, 1962, the AMS officially turned down the Washington course. The reasons given for this were that Stephenson had begun teaching at St. Joseph's School for the Deaf in the Bronx, New York; that envisioned demonstration class teacher also had other commitments; fiscally it was not feasible; and finally, only fourteen of the applicants who had ultimately registered had college degrees (the minimum AMS requirement). A telegram expressing AMS' belief that a course could not be run with a limited number of personnel without jeopardizing AMS teaching standards was sent to Margaret Stephenson. Also, the State Department was contacted as to the non-employment status of her AMS-sponsored visa.

A week later (September 12), however, Washington representatives requested to attend an Executive Committee meeting to further air their views on the feasibility of a Washington training course. They stated they were willing to work within the AMS framework and thought it financially possible. AMS agreed to reopen its study of the matter. At the same meeting, a telegram was read from Mario Montessori to the Board of AMS stating, "If Miss Stephenson not reassumed as course trainer provisional agreement AMS and AMI becomes void and AMI will feel free to recognize courses not run by AMS."[51]

The controversy over this course continued. Mother Isabel, a member of the Pedagogical Committee, at a meeting on September 15, insisted it was the obligation of the AMS Board to see that a course was provided if there were interest in it and acceptable to the Pedagogical Committee. AMS said only if it were financially feasible. Again on September 17, 1962, the Executive Committee reaffirmed the same position it had taken at all of its meetings. In so doing, they expressed their feelings that this Washington course would hinder "the effective grafting of Montessori insights into acceptance by the American educational system at the highest and most respected level."[52]

The Washington group decided to go ahead with a course without AMS approval and to work actively with Margaret Stephenson, who became the course trainer. The AMS sent a message to Dr. James Egan, head of the Washington group, condemning this action. A follow-up letter was sent to Mario advising him of the situation and informing him of a telegram that had been sent to Miss Stephenson, urging that a personality schism not be allowed to split the American Montessori movement.

The AMS was greatly concerned as to what effect this action would have on the implantation of the Montessori Method into the American educational system, and its effect on their functioning as sole representative of the AMI in America. In addition to the course, this position had already been threatened by Mario Montessori in his telegram referring to the rehiring of Miss Stephenson and in a letter in which he indicated that the AMS was not living up to the tentative agreement to give all courses recommended by AMI using all AMI recommended personnel. All attempts to ease misunderstanding with both Margaret Stephenson and Mario Montessori were not effective.

On October 11, AMS received a telegram from Dr. James Egan, head of the Washington Montessori group informing them they were "proceeding with pedagogically sound training course in full accord with the precepts advocated by AMS Pedagogical Committee and Mario Montessori." They warned AMS, "Further ill-considered retaliatory action by AMS can only cause impediment to effective development of Montessori in America."[53]

Since they had received no official communication from AMI, the AMS continued to function as AMI's representative.

In addition to teacher training problems, AMS was having severe financial difficulties. In 1962, Douglas Gravel arrived at the AMS office and found a mimeograph company representative attempting to reclaim their machine for lack of payment. Aware of the absolute necessity of it to the furthering of the society, Douglas paid the bill with his and Maria Gravel's personal check.[54]

The Board discussed a great variety of ideas for obtaining more money and for becoming a strong national organization. The steps for launching the Montessori Movement into the American educational structure were carefully planned. James Ruffing concluded they must realize there is an element of business involved but it cannot be applied absolutely. He felt Montessori education was a real good idea on which they must gamble. They must get the people in the field to realize AMS was not a fly-by-night organization. The Executive Committee discussed if it were realistic for the AMS to continue to function under the current fiscal conditions. The consensus of opinion was that AMS should continue and that it must "institutionalize" as a service organization.

Extreme financial difficulties compelled AMS to act immediately to insert Montessori ideals into the American educational picture. Frederick Ossorio stated, "AMS is being forced to concentrate its total resources, intellectual and fiscal, on the specific contribution it can make to American education derived from Montessori insights and to pin its hopes on the relevance of this program for a breakthrough in recognition and acceptance."[55]

Because of the crucial difference between the AMS's goal to insert Montessori insights into the American culture as opposed to the goal of the AMI to simply establish Montessori schools in the United States, the differences in outlook on teacher training, and the trans-oceanic control of the organization with its inherent financial agreement, relations between AMS and AMI were becoming more and more strained. However, each party still felt some need for the other. AMS attempted to discuss their differences in a letter on September 27, 1962 to Mario Montessori. Their letter dealt with AMS-AMI aims, courses and trainees, the status of Margaret Stephenson, the financial agreement between AMS and AMI, and other misunderstandings.

In November 1962, Mario Montessori responded that he had always sought to foster trust and confidence between AMS and AMI. He said that it was he who had insisted on the formation of AMS with enough authority to insure the future of the Montessori Movement in America and had always stood solidly in support of the AMS. He concluded, "Why should I wish to destroy something that I have worked so hard to create?[56] He then elaborated on the conditions necessary for the ratification of the AMI-AMS agreement; the crux of this was the necessity to keep Margaret Stephenson as a trainer. He added that he chose to ignore the causes behind the Washington situation and "if AMI were officially consulted it would be bound to recognize the Washington course and deny recognition to the Greenwich one."[57] He appealed for conciliation efforts between AMS and the Washington group.

As indicated, these overt differences were the result of deeper underlying factors. The November 17 meeting of the Pedagogical Committee pointed up some of the real questions at issue between AMS and AMI in regard to American educational policy. The problem of testing was introduced. Nancy indicated that one of the first questions Americans pose is what research has been done to prove Montessori education is better than anything that exists. She said it was necessary to obtain an inventory of what American children can do at age three and what are American parents' and society's expectations of a child of this age. Also, it was necessary to know what American children do in first grade in order to fulfill requirements of state educational laws.

The issue of ancillary courses related to American educational goals and values was another one of the steps to establish the Montessori Movement in the United States as an American phenomenon. These courses were added to the 1962 Greenwich program, taught by Professor John McDermott of City University of New York.

Nancy Rambusch resigned as President of the AMS on November 7, 1962, effective June 30, 1963. The minutes which reported this resignation also carried the following statement:

> There seemed to be an implied paradox that in the process of depersonalizing the Montessori movement, there nevertheless was a need for personalities, wherever they may be found, whose sense of vocation was viewed, not as a focal point for personal ambition, but only as objective instruments in the service of the larger cause. It is conceivable that such impersonal personalities as members of the new management group might evoke the hopes of realizing through their instrumentality the potentialities seen in the Montessori content.[58]

The inference of this statement, when examined in connection with statements in the press and journals of that time, indicates the Montessori movement had become associated with Nancy McCormick Rambusch, as its personal representative, rather than with the AMS and the phenomena of Montessori education as a social movement. AMS saw the need to depersonalize and in so doing emphasize the content of the Montessori principles and their value to the American educational scene.

I questioned Nancy about this statement and she indicated her resignation was linked to the fact that she did not feel the need for the personal advancement implied in the statement but preferred to step down to give the movement a chance to grow and to gain financial support divorced from personality problems.[59]

In a letter to Mario Montessori, Nancy expressed similar ideas very strongly. She wrote:

> As you may have noticed, from the Minutes, I am tendering my resignation, as the principal executive officer of the American Montessori Society, this coming July. This year, for the first tune, I received renumeration (sic) from the Montessori Society. In years past, I received none. I would prefer a relationship in which I could help in whatever way possible without continuing to assume the problems and absorb all the abuse that has been showered on me from every quarter. I believe that I have proven my loyalty to the ideals of the Montessori

movement in a more definitive way than perhaps anyone else in this country. It would have been easy for me, ten years ago, to have returned from Europe and submerged the name of Montessori and promoted these ideas in some other way. It was not my intent then to do so. I think this would be a criminal neglect of the genius of Dr. Montessori, as well as an intellectually dishonest move. I continue to believe this to be the case, and yet I cannot help ponder the fact that many of the outstanding people who have become interested in Montessori in the past, have turned away in disgust when they have seen the petty politicking that exists at the heart of this movement. I would not pursue their course; I would only say that I have given the Montessori Society, not only my own time, but that of my husband and children, over almost a decade.[60]

By mid-December 1962, the time of this letter, relations between AMS and AMI had almost completely broken down. In order to preserve that which existed and move forward, Nancy set up an AMS Interim Operating Committee composed of William T. Hanley, Ronald Koegler, M.D., and Robert Higgins. This group sent letters to Mario Montessori, James Egan (Washington Group) and Margaret Stephenson. They wrote it was their purpose to clear up misunderstandings between AMS and AMI, and to resolve differences within AMS itself. "Also, by relieving Mrs. Rambusch from many of the administrative duties which she has been burdened she will be freed for the pedagogical and leadership roles which pressure of time has not permitted her."[61]

Mario Montessori wrote to Nancy, turning down her request to come to Europe to see him because he felt their meetings, although pleasant, were never productive. On December 19, she tried once again to respond to some of the questions raised by Montessori in reference to the training courses and the pedagogical committee. She concluded her letter:

I will make no further effort to see you. I think perhaps time will vindicate the validity of many of the comments I have made to you. In our own time we may not see the implication of the work that has been started in America. Hopefully, Montessori can remain, as Dr. John McDermott has said, "a residual influence in American education," something that in its first appearance here, it was not able to become.[62]

On January 11, 1963, Mario Montessori informed the Interim Operating Committee that the Executive Committee of AMI had decided not to recognize AMS courses exclusively, i.e., they would now recognize the Washington training course.[63] AMS reported back to him on the discussions of their January 19, 1963 meeting, informing him that their legal counsel had advised them that the Pedagogical Committee was no longer in effect since it was selected by AMI, and AMS was no longer the sole representative of the AMI in America.[64]

The AMS continued to emphasize the value of Montessori's insights for American society. In March, 1963, they published a paper called *AMS Information Items*. It explained its purpose as a service publication for all AMS members and as an instrument to facilitate integration of the Montessori Method into American culture. Its content would not be limited to strictly Montessori-oriented materials or to any "monolithic" interpretation of the Montessori movement, and non-Montessori publications, which are either consistent with her insights or which extend them in terms of current theories and data for the American Montessori classroom and American culture would be included.[65] The first issue carried a reprint of a book review by John McDermott of Nancy McCormick Rambusch's book, *Learning How to Learn: An American Approach to Montessori* and E.M. Standing's book, *The Montessori Method: A Revolution in Education*. Once again, McDermott advised Americans to look at Montessori with a more egalitarian view.

One month later, on April 25, 1963, Mario Montessori wrote to Robert Higgins, his representative to AMS and a member of the Interim Operating committee, telling him AMS was still the representative of AMI, but that they were no longer the sole group responsible for teacher training in the United States. He then enumerated the conditions necessary for a group to be an AMI representative and indicated that AMS did not meet these conditions. However, contradictorily, he also indicated AMI would be willing to examine students enrolled in the Greenwich course for certification if AMS paid for the expenses in advance.[66]

After a great deal of personal correspondence between Nancy and Mario and Mario and the Interim Operating Committee, Nancy and Mario finally brought their arguments to Montessorians; Nancy in the first issue of *The AMS Bulletin* and Mario in *A Long Letter to Montessorians in America*. Nancy reiterated her reasons for moving beyond Montessori's original insights to accommodate American culture. She repeated the desire to make teacher training and curriculum development relevant. She concluded, "To the question which Susan E. Blow addressed to those who "dared" to question her master, Fredrich Froebel, 'Do you think you can improve on what he did?' The answer is 'yes' in the context of its application to American children, the AMS certainly does think it can improve on Montessori practice."[67]

Mario, too, restated his position with regard to teacher training and the Pedagogical Committee in the United States. He recognized Nancy's central role in the re-introduction of Montessori to America but warned against "neo-Montessorians who too hastily try to put into practice seemingly logical and marvelous additions." He pleaded, "Let us be humans and not penguins, who, if they find an orphan chick, try to take possession of it in order to mother it and, in doing, so pull him apart."[68] Mario was still willing to work with AMS and indicated, "AMI and I do not wish to deny or split from AMS, but if AMS creates a split then God Bless them."[69]

In addition he did not criticize Nancy Rambusch and the AMS because he was resolved to make Montessori last in America. He wrote, "I, who founded it (AMI) with Dr. Montessori swore to myself that I would not rest if it took my whole life to do it until Montessori was brought back to all the countries where Dr. Montessori had worked, suffered and had been expelled." The letter continued, "It has taken all my life, but AMI has done it. The last two countries were Spain and America. In both a first step has been made, and in America, do not forget it was through the courage and determination of Mrs. Rambusch."[70]

All attempts at reconciliation were of no avail and on November 28, 1963, Mario Montessori officially resigned from the American Montessori Society Board.[71]

As we approach the fiftieth anniversary of the American Montessori Society, it is important to explore the reasons why Montessori education in the United States has survived and thrived after its founder, Nancy McCormick Rambusch, no longer served as the charismatic leader and figurehead of the movement.

During a taping in 1986, Douglas Gravel and Bretta Weiss explored some of these reasons. It was their belief that Nancy, who might not have expected the AMS to flourish after her departure, had left a self-selected Board of Directors who were very strong. They had the motivation and ability to guide and sustain the newly-formed organization. Douglas Gravel indicated that Nancy always sought individuals whose opinions she valued before making any weighty decisions. He implied there were times she subtly persuaded them to go along with her interpretations, but she did listen to the ideas of others and integrate them into her final resolutions.

In 1963, just before Nancy left the Presidency, the American Montessori Society's office was in a highly disorganized state. Part time attention was being given to the mail, the files, and phone calls. The focus was on spreading the movement and handling the conflicts between AMS and AMI. Once again, Douglas Gravel stepped in and helped resolve an immediate need of the organization. He sought the help of one of his mother's lifelong friends and a friend of his entire family, Cleo Henrietta Monson. She had worked in many office positions in the past and was not happy with her position at that time. Therefore, she was persuaded to leave her job and come to Greenwich, Connecticut to work with the AMS.

When Cleo began work in January 1963, the society was already in its third year. It was $11,000 in the red, the office was poorly managed and there were cartons of unanswered letters from people wanting to start Montessori schools. She was hired to make order out of chaos. In addition, she was to manage the teacher-training and visitation programs. Cleo handled all of these tasks with efficiency and good common sense. Her salary was $165 a week until they gave her a room in the back of the office where she could sleep and work until midnight rather than commute to New York City. Thereupon, her salary was reduced by $15.00 a week and rarely paid on time. In August 1963, at Cleo's insistence, the office moved to New York City.

As the organization grew, she oversaw an office staff and a Montessori materials and publications center. This center was another vision of Douglas Gravel's. Foreseeing the need for materials by the burgeoning number of new schools in America, he ordered materials that he and his wife paid for out of their own pockets and supplied them for the schools.

Until 1969, Cleo also handled the finances of AMS in collaboration with the treasurer. Some of the additional tasks she undertook were building up a Montessori library, working with Montessori teacher activities, coordinating the visitation programs and teacher-training courses and disseminating information to the public on Montessori.[72]

James Ruffing, President of AMS, June 1963–June 1969 described Cleo's leadership, "Miss Monson has maintained–by skill, intelligence, determination, self-sacrifice and an enormous amount of work above and beyond mere duties—a national central AMS office. This contribution to Montessori on her part is distinctive in view of the fact that it has been partially and often substantially because of this work that so many others in and outside of AMS have been able to supply their own valuable contributions."[73] Cleo Monson's organizational leadership was a major factor in sustaining the Montessori movement in the United States. Ten years after she began working at AMS, Cleo was named its first National Director.

But, it was Nancy's prior leadership skills that had established the foundation for the subsequent years that followed her resignation. In her dissertation, Nancy described her prior lack of knowledge about innovation and change. She wrote, "I was innocent of the literature on 'change,' 'change agents,' and what little there was on 'change agentry.' If anyone had called me an 'opinion leader' or a 'diffuser,' I would not have known whether to be flattered or insulted."[74] Her innate perceptions led her in the direction which feminist leaders would discover decades later when they were searching for ways to make inroads into male dominated societies. One of her best insights was to grasp the moment in time and the sub-culture that was ripe for change. She called it "psychic franchise." She clearly understood the impact the Russian satellite Sputnik, in combination with dissatisfaction with Catholic parochial schools, could play in the revival of Montessori education in the United States. Her own perceived need for a better education for her son led her to women who had the same need and the desire to promote a program that would alleviate their anxieties about a good education for their children.

Although the circumstances were the impetus for the introduction of a new educational system, change required vision, energy, support, time and collaboration. Nancy had the vision and energy, and she would give of her time, but she needed both financial and moral support. The young educated Catholic community would provide her with both. Her article in *Jubilee* set the stage for the rebirth of the Montessori movement.

In retrospect, having learned the terminology of the change agent, Nancy quoted Sarason who believed the success or failure of any change was dependent upon "some combination of a single individual's temperament, intellect and motivation," but he also believed in the Zeitgeist. Nancy believed she used a combination of both.[75] Cremin proposed one definition of a change agent might be "committed nut."[76] Commenting on this definition, Nancy wrote if this is "critical to change, then I was the perfect choice for the diffusion of American Montessori education. I was single-minded and persuaded that Montessori had to have an American formulation. I was innovative, creative, searching for something new and dissatisfied with the status quo."[77] Her intuition told her that the education of young children needed to be changed, and she would be the one to do it. She had located individuals with the same felt need as she, but through her voracious reading she knew she had to have more collaboration. She found it in the person of John McDermott who helped her to put Montessori into an American context.

Nancy's dissertation described what she learned about change models, after the fact. She wrote that initially she utilized the "center-periphery model, which she described "as person A telling person B something new to person B."[78] This model has two variants; the Johnny Appleseed and the Magnet. She employed the Johnny Appleseed variant "in which an innovator traverses the field with his new message, gathering adherents as he travels."[79]

As the American Montessori Society developed, so did the strategies. Unlike the original Montessori model, which retained the center-periphery prototype, a "proliferation of centers" model evolved where regional centers became their own peripheral points. Different teacher- training centers around the country utilized their own modalities of diffusing the method, guided by the home organization. Montessori education in this interpretation became an American phenomenon. Nancy described it as "transmutation rather than transplantation."[80] Although the conflict between AMS and AMI dealt with many other issues, this was the crux of their disputes. Americanization of the Montessori Method and Nancy's leadership in encouraging and developing this variant in a diverse culture has sustained the Montessori movement in the United States today.

Introduction of the Montessori Method to public schools began with a strong ethical impetus in American society. The long-awaited desegregation mandated by Brown vs. the Board of Education in 1954 prompted the beginnings of Magnet Schools about two decades later. The story of the introduction of Montessori education to the public schools can be found in Chapter 3 where the incremental planned change is described. This change was intentional not intuitive. Nancy carefully applied the change agentry strategies she had studied. This she insisted was to be a Montessori public school, not a public Montessori school, similar to her statement years before that it would be the American Montessori Society and not the Montessori American Society. It was not an easy transition for teachers trained in public elementary school curriculum and methods. Nancy saw "first hand the complexity and peril that change efforts face in entrenched organizations."[81] She persevered, utilizing formal goal setting and policies. She demonstrated flexibility and willingness to share power with the teachers and principals involved in the change. All of these strategies later identified by a variety of authors as women's leadership skills enabled the early vision of Montessori public education by Nancy and John McDermott to begin to take hold in American society.

Nancy also employed at least five of Bornstein's six qualities necessary for social entrepreneurs or, as I have termed it, leadership skills. She demonstrated willingness to self-correct, willingness to share credit, willingness to break free of established structures, willingness to cross disciplinary boundaries, and had strong ethical impetus."[82] However, I don't think I ever saw Nancy "work quietly" which is the sixth quality. Her voice was her strength.

Although Nancy obviously did not do it single-handedly, her early struggles helped establish a social movement entrenching private Montessori schools in America as we know them, while, her later efforts set the model for the public and charter schools that are growing in the United States today.

NOTES

1. In a List of Experimental and Progressive Schools of the Bureau of Educational Experiments only two Montessori schools are mentioned. The Child Education Foundation is one of them. In: Agnes DeLima, *Our Enemy the Child*, (New York: New Republic, Inc., 1926).
2. http://nobelprize.org/nomination/peace/ retrieved March 21, 2009.
3. Bernard Iddings Bell, *Crisis in Education, Challenge to American Complacency*, (New York: McGraw-Hill Book Co., Inc., 1949), 10. A parallel study of this criticism can be found in Lawrence A. Cremin, *The Transformation of the School,* (New York: Vintage Books, 1961), 333–347.

4. Mortimer Smith, *And Madly Teach*, (Chicago: Henry Regnery Co., 1949), 105.

5. Bell, *Crisis in Education,* 31—35.

6. Arthur Bestor, *Educational Wastelands: The Retreat from Learning in Our Public Schools,* (Urbana: The University of Illinois Press, 1953), 10.

7. Hollis L. Caswell, "The Great Reappraisal of Public Education," *Teachers College Record*, 54 (October, 1952):12 and 13–19. See also Mary Anne Raywid, *The Ax-Grinders* (New York: The Macmillan Co., 1962).

8. Nancy McCormick Rambusch, "Montessori Insights and American Children Today," *Catholic Reporter*, (Section II, May 31, 1963): 10.

9. Ibid.

10. Interview with Nancy McCormick Rambusch, Greenwich, Connecticut, July 8, 1970.

11. Nancy McCormick Rambusch, "Letter to Mario Montessori," (November 19, 1956), 2–3. AMS files. Rambusch credited the major merchandising strategy for selling educational toys in the 1960's to the intuition of Frank Kaplan, president of Creative Playthings. She indicated that he took advantage of the anxiety provoked by Sputnik to give the child a head start with good toys. Interview with Nancy McCormick Rambusch, July 8, 1970.

12. Ada Montessori, "Letter to Mrs. Robert Rambusch," (December 20, 1956), 1. AMS files.

13. Nancy McCormick Rambusch, "Learning Made Easy," *Jubilee*, (I, September, 1953): 47.

14. "Unsigned letter to prominent Greenwich, Connecticut citizens," (November 24, 1958). Whitby School files. I was unable to ascertain the author of this letter.

15. "Montessori Information Items," prepared by the Cleveland Montessori Association. (New York: American Montessori Society): 25.

16. Ibid.

17. Whitescarver and Cossentino, "Montessori and the Mainstream," 2583.

18. John J. McDermott, "Montessori and the New America," in *Building the Foundations of Learning*, (New York: American Montessori Society, 1963): 25.

19. Ibid., 28.

20. Mario Montessori, "Letter to Mrs. Robert E. Rambusch," (June 15, 1959), AMS files.

21. Nancy McCormick Rambusch, "Letter to Mario Montessori," (February 29, 1960), AMS files.

22. Mario Montessori, "Letter to Nancy McCormick Rambusch," (June 19, 1959), AMS files.

23. Nancy McCormick Rambusch, "Letter to the United States Immigration and Naturalization Service," (n.d.), AMS files.

24. R. Joosten-Chutzen, General Secretary, AMI, "Letter to the President of AMS," (November 9, 1960). AMS files.

25. The American Montessori Society, Inc., "Minutes of the first meeting of Incorporators," (May 22, 1961). AMS files.

26. "Minutes of the Council Meeting of the Association Montessori Internationale," (August 5, 1961), 3, AMS files.
27. Thomas W. Hayes, "Letter to J. Patrick Rooney, Jr.," (December 15, 1961), 1–2, AMS files.
28. Nancy McCormick Rambusch, "American Montessori Society Minutes of Informal Board Meeting," (April 9, 1962), AMS files.
29. Ibid., 2.
30. Ibid.
31. "Calendar of Events with Reference to Organization of AMS Course in Washington, D.C.," (1962), 1. AMS files.
32. Ibid.
33. Nancy McCormick Rambusch, Tape Recording, AMS Seminar, Greenwich, Connecticut, (June 4, 1962), AMS office.
34. Mario Montessori, Ibid.
35. Rambusch, Ibid.
36. Mario Montessori, Ibid.
37. Ibid.
38. Rambusch, Ibid.
39. Ibid.
40. Mario Montessori, Ibid.
41. Ibid.
42. Ibid.
43. Robert Higgins, Tape Recording, AMS Seminar, Greenwich, CT, (June 7, 1962), AMS Office.
44. Sally Cassidy, Tape Recording, AMS Seminar, Greenwich, CT, (June 1962), AMS Office.
45. "Calendar of Events," 3.
46. Alfred Gottschalk, Hebrew Union College, "Letter to Mrs. Nancy McCormick Rambusch," (July 30, 1962), AMS files.
47. "Minutes of the Whitby School Board Meeting," (July 23, 1962), 1. Whitby School files.
48. Philip M. Drake, "Letter to Nancy McCormick Rambusch," (July 27, 1962), 2. Whitby files.
49. James Egan, M.D., "Letter to the Board of Directors, American Montessori Society," (July 12, 1962). AMS files.
50. "Minutes of the AMS Executive Committee Meeting," (July 20, 1962). AMS files.
51. "Minutes of the AMS Executive Board Meeting," (September 12, 1962). AMS files.
52. "Minutes of the AMS Executive Committee Meeting," (September 17, 1962). AMS files.
53. James W. Egan, "Telegram to the Executive Committee of AMS," (October 11, 1962). AMS files.

54. Douglas Gravel, transcribed DVD from personal collection of Maria and Douglas Gravel, (1986). Copy given to me by Marie Dugan. Currently in AMS Archives, Storrs, Connecticut.

55. Frederic Ossorio, "Minutes of the AMS Executive Committee," (August 23, 1962), 2. AMS files.

56. Mario Montessori, "Letter to the Board of the American Montessori Society," (November, 1962), 1. AMS files.

57. Ibid., 3–4.

58. "Minutes of the AMS Executive Committee," (November 7, 1962), 5–6. AMS files.

59. Conversation with Nancy McCormick Rambusch, December 5, 1970.

60. Nancy McCormick Rambusch, "Letter to Mario Montessori," (December 19, 1962). AMS files.

61. AMS Interim Operating Committee, "Letter to Mario Montessori," (December 14, 1962), 1, AMS files.

62. Nancy McCormick Rambusch, "Letter to Mario Montessori," (December 19, 1962), 4. AMS files.

63. Mario Montessori, "Letter to the American Montessori Society, Interim Operating Committee," (January 11, 1963). AMS files.

64. AMS Board of Directors, "Letter to Mario Montessori," (January 21, 1963), 1. AMS files.

65. AMS Information Items, 1, (March 1963), AMS files.

66. Mario Montessori, "Letter to Robert Higgins," (April 25, 1963), 4 pages, AMS files.

67. Nancy McCormick Rambusch, *The AMS Bulletin*, (I, no.1, 1963), 2.

68. Mario Montessori, "A Long Letter to Montessorians," 10–11.

69. Ibid., 11.

70. Ibid., 5.

71. "Minutes of the AMS Board Meeting," (January 18–19, 1964), 2, AMS files.

72. Observations and conversations with Cleo Monson, (April 1970–May 1971).

73. James Ruffing, Telephone interview with author, (May 17, 1971).

74. Nancy McCormick Rambusch, *Intuitive and Intentional Change*, 3.

75. Ibid., 8–9.

76. Quoted in Rambusch, Ibid., 42.

77. Rambusch, Ibid., 49–50.

78. Rambusch, Ibid., 54.

79. Ibid., 55.

80. Conversation with Nancy McCormick Rambusch, June 1970.

81. Nancy McCormick Rambusch, *Intuitive and Intentional Change*, 174.

82. David Bornstein, *How to Change the World*, 233–239.

Selected Bibliography

Alpern, Sara, Joyce Antler, Elizabeth Israels Perry and Ingrid Winther Scobie. *The Challenge of Feminist Biography: Writing the Lives of Modern American Women.* Urbana, Illinois: University of Illinois Press, 1992.

Antler, Joyce and Sara Knopp Biklen. *Changing Education: Women as Radicals and Conservators.* Albany: State University of New York Press, 1990.

Astin, Helen S. and Carole Leland. Women of Influence, Women of Vision: A Cross *Generational Study of Leaders and Change.* San Francisco: Jossey-Bass Publishers, 1991.

Babini, Valeria. "Science, Feminism and Education: the Early Work of Maria Montessori. *History Workshop Journal* 29 (Spring 2000): 45–67.

Babini, Valeria and Luisa Lama. *Una Donna Nuova: Il Femminismo scientifico di Maria Montessori.* Milano, Italy: Franco Angeli, 2000.

Barnett, H.G. *Innovation the Basis of Cultural Change.* New York: McGraw Hill Book Co, Inc., 1953.

Bateson, Mary Catherine. *Composing a Life.* New York: A Plume Book, 1990.

Beineke, John A. *And There Were Giants in the Land: The Life of William Heard Kilpatrick.* New York: Peter Lang, 1998.

Bell, Bernard Iddings. *Crisis in Education, Challenge to American Complacency.* New York: McGraw Hill Book Co. Inc., 1949.

Bestor, Arthur. *Educational Wastelands: The Retreat from Learning in Our Public Schools,* Urbana: The University of Illinois Press., 1953.

Boggs, L. Pearl. "The Eternally Feminine in the Montessori System." *American Childhood* (May 1917): 195–196.

Bornstein, David. *How to Change the World: Social Entrepreneurs and the Power of New Ideas.* New York: Oxford University Press, 2004.

Bortolotti, Franca Pieroni. *Alle origini del movimento Femminile in Italia: 1848–1892.* Turin, Italy: Giulio Einaudi Editore, 1963.

——. *Sul Movimento Politico Delle Donne.* Rome: Utopia, 1987.

——. "A Survey of Recent Italian Research on the History of Feminism." *The Journal of Italian History* 1 (Winter 1978): 511–530.

Bourque, Susan C. and Donna Robinson Divine, eds. *Women Living Change*. Philadelphia: Temple University Press, 1985.

Brubacher, John S. *A History of Problems of Education*. New York: McGraw Hill Book Co., 1966.

Buckenmeyer, Robert G., editor. *The California Lectures of Maria Montessori*. Oxford, England: Clio Press, 1997.

Carlson, Richard O. *Adoption of Educational Innovations*. Eugene, Oregon: The Center for the Advanced Study of Educational Administration, 1965.

——. *Change Processes in Public Schools*. Eugene, Oregon: University of Oregon, 1965.

Cather, Willa. *The Autobiography of S.S. McClure*. Lincoln, Nebraska: University of Nebraska Press, 1997.

Chattin-McNichols, John. *The Montessori Controversy*. Albany, New York: Delmar Publishers, 1992.

Collier, Richard. *Duce! A Biography of Benito Mussolini*. New York: Viking Press, 1971.

Cusack, Ginny. "Building Ukrainian Montessori from the Ground Up." *Montessori Life* 20, 2, (2008): 22–27.

DeFelice, Renzo. *Mussolini il duce: Gli Anni del consenso, 1929–1936*. Turin, Italy: Giulio Einaudi Editors, 1974.

DeGrazia, Victoria. *How Fascism Ruled Women: Italy, 1922–1945*. Berkeley, California: University of California Press, 1992.

Der internationale Kongress fur Frauenwerke und Frauenbestrebungen in Berlin. 19 bis *26* September 1896, Berlin: 1897.

Durham, Martin. *Women and Fascism*. London: Routledge, 1998.

Farley, Jane Mary. "Milwaukeean Leads Revolution in Three R's," *The Milwaukee Journal* (October 8, 1961): 4–5.

Fermi, Laura. *Mussolini*. Chicago: University of Chicago Press, 1961.

Flynn, Mary C. "Headmistress." *Today: National Catholic Magazine*. (November 1961): 3–5.

Freeman, Sue J.M., Susan Bourque and Christine Shelton. *Women on Power: Leadership Redefined*. Boston: Northeastern University Press, 2001.

Gallo, Max. *Mussolini's Italy: Twenty Years of the Fascist Era*. New York: Macmillan Publishing Company, 1964.

Grossman, Lee. *The Change Agent*. New York: Amacom, 1974.

Halperin, William S. *Mussolini and Italian Fascism*. Princeton, NJ: D. Van Nostrand Company, Inc., 1964.

Heilbrun, Carolyn. *Writing A Woman's Life*. New York: Ballantine Books, 1988.

Helgesen, Sally. *The Female Advantage: Women's Ways of Leadership*. New York: Doubleday Currency, 1990.

Hurd-Mead, Kate Campbell. *A History of Women in Medicine*. Haddam, CT: The Haddam Press, 1938.

Holtby, Winifred. *The Land of Green Ginger*, Chicago: Cassandra Editions, 1978.

Iles, Teresa, ed. *All Sides of the Subject: Women and Biography*. New York: Teachers College Press, 1992.

Kennedy, Mary, et.al. *Making Connections: Women's Studies, Women's Movements, Women's Lives*. London: Taylor & Francis, 1993.

Kolb, Judith A. "Are We Still Stereotyping Leadership? A Look at Gender and Other Predictors of Leader Emergence." *Small Group Research*, 28, 3 (August 1997): 370–393.

Koon, Tracy H. *Believe, Obey, Fight: Political Socialization of Youth in Fascist Italy*. Chapel Hill, NC: University of North Carolina Press, 1985.

Kramer, Rita. *Maria Montessori: A Biography*. New York: G.P. Putnam's Sons, 1976.

Leeds, Christopher. *Italy Under Mussolini*. London: Wayland Publishers, 1972.

Loeffler, Margaret, ed. *Montessori in Contemporary American Culture*. Portsmouth, NH: Heinemann Educational Books, Inc., 1992.

Lovejoy, Esther Pohl. *Women Doctors of the World*. New York: The Macmillan Co., 1957.

Lyon, Peter. *The Life and Times of S.S. McClure*. New York: Charles Scribner's Sons, 1963.

Maccheroni, Anna Maria. *A True Romance: Dr. Montessori as I Knew Her*. Edinburgh: The Darien Press, n.d.

MacGregor-Hastie, *The Day of the Lion: The Life and Death of Fascist Italy, 1922–1945*. New York: Coward-McCann, Inc., 1963.

Maria Montessori: A Centenary Anthology: 1870–1970. Association Montessori Internationale, 1970.

Maynard, Mary and June Purvis. *Researching Women's Lives from a Feminist Perspective*. London: Taylor & Francis, Ltd., 1994.

McClure, S.S. The Autobiography of S.S. McClure. Lincoln: University of Nebraska Press, 1997.

Merrill, Jenny B. "A New Method in Infant Education." *The Kindergarten Primary Magazine*. Five articles in series (Beginning December 1909).

Montessori, Maria. E*ducation for a New World*. Adyar, Madras, India: Kalakshetra Publications, 1963.

Montessori, Mario. "A Long Letter to Montessorians in America in Answer to Some of the Many Questions I Receive." Amsterdam: M.J. Portielje, (1963): 1–11.

Morley, Louise and Val Walsh, *Breaking Boundaries: Women in Higher Education*. London: Taylor and Francis, 1996.

Mozans, H.J., *Woman in Science*. Notre Dame, Indiana: University of Notre Dame, 1991.

Murphy, Mary Beth. "Scratch Parent, Find Educator." *The Milwaukee Sentinel (*May 24, 1978): 9–10.

Payne, Charles. "Ella Baker and Models of Social Change" *Signs 14, 4* (Summer 1989):892–896.

Personal Narratives Group, eds. *Interpreting Women's Lives*. Bloomington, Indiana: Indiana University Press, 1989.

Pickering-Iazzi, Robin, ed., *Mothers of Invention: Women, Italian Fascism, and Culture*. Minneapolis: University of Minnesota Press, 1995.

Rambusch, Nancy McCormick. "Children's House: The Social System."(June, 1977): AMS Archives, Teachers College, Special Collections.

———. "Facing the Montessori Challenge as Americans." Speech, (June 15, 1963): AMS Archives, Teachers College, Special Collections, Box 9, Series 7.3, Folder 7.

———. *Intuitive and Intentional Change Agentry.* Unpublished Doctoral Dissertation. University of Massachusetts: (1977).

———. *Learning How to Learn.* Baltimore: Helicon Press, Inc., 1962.

———. "Learning Made Easy." *Jubilee*, I (September 1953): 46–53.

———. "The Modern Montessori Approach," *American Montessori Society Bulletin* 8, 1: (1970).

———. "Montessori as an American Public School Alternative," *The Constructive Triangle* 3, 1: (Spring 1976).

———. "Montessori for American Children," New York: Montessori Materials Center: (1963). AMS Archives, Teachers College, Special Collections, Box 9, Series 7.3, Folder 7.

———. "Montessori's Flawed Diffusion Model: An American Montessori Diffusion Philosophy." ERIC Document ED352204 (1992): 1–6.

———. "Speech," (September, 1962). AMS Archives, Box 9, Series 7.3, Folder 7, Teachers College, Special Collections.

———. "The American Montessori Experience." *The American Montessori Society Bulletin* 15, 2, (1977).

———. "The American Montessori Picture—Some Reconsiderations," *The American Montessori Society Bulletin* 1, 1, (1963).

———. "The New Generation of Montessori Schools." (November 14, 1981). AMS Archives, Teachers College, Special Collections.

———. "Woman and Catholic in 1986," Speech: (May 7, 1986).

Rhode, Deborah L. *The Difference "Difference" Makes: Women and Leadership.* Stanford, CA: Stanford University Press, 2003.

Riger, Stephanie. "Challenges of Success: Stages of Growth in Feminist Organizations." *Feminist Studies* 20, 2 (Summer 1994): 275–300.

Rusch, Edith A. Penny Poplin Gosetti and Marge Mohoric. "The Social Construction of Leadership: Theory to Praxis." ERIC Document EA024265 (November 1991): 1–24.

Schneider, Howard W. *The Fascist Government of Italy.* New York: D. Van Nostrand Company, 1936.

Schwegman, Marjan. *Maria Montessori.* Bologna, Italy: Il Mulino, 1999, In Italian.

Smith, Denis Mack. *Italy.* New York: Alfred A. Knopf, 1982.

Sochen, June. *Movers and Shakers: American Women Thinkers and Activists: 1900–1970.* New York: Quadrangle/The New York Times Book Co., 1973.

Standing, E., ed... *The Child in the Church by Maria Montessori and others*, St. Paul, Minnesota: Catechical Guild, 1965.

Stanley, L. and Wise, S. *Breaking Out: Feminist Consciousness and Feminist Research.* London: Routledge & Kegan Paul, 1983.

Tannenbaum, Edward R. *The Fascist Experience: Italian Society and Culture, 1922–1945.* New York: Basic Books, 1972.

Tenenbaum, Samuel. *William Heard Kilpatrick: Trail Blazers in Education*. New York: Harper and Brothers Publishers, 1951.

Tilly, Louise A. and Patricia Gurin, eds. *Women, Politics, and Change*. New York: Russell Sage Foundation, 1990.

Time. "Return of Montessori."15, 5 (February 3, 1930): cover, 36, 29–39.

Time. "The Joy of Learning," May 12, 1961, 63–64.

Tonzig, Maria. "Quaderni Per La Storia Dell'Universita di Padova." Padova, Italy: Atenore: 1973: 182–193.

Tozier, Josephine. "An Educational Wonder Worker- The Methods of Maria Montessori." *McClure's Magazine*: Entire Series beginning (May 1911).

Wagner-Martin, Linda. *Telling Women's Lives: The New Biography*. New Brunswick, NJ: Rutgers University Press, 1994.

Wilson, Perry R. *The Clockwork Factory: Women and Work in Fascist Italy*. Oxford: Clarendon Press, 1993.

Index